SONAS

Celtic Thoughts on Happiness

Catherine Conlon has a degree in Medicine and is a lecturer in Public Health at UCC. Her keen interest in matters health-related gave rise to the idea for a book that would explore the depths beneath the superficial distractions of modern Irish life: consumerism and noise. A mother of four living in Cork, she cites winning the Young Scientist Exhibition as a schoolgirl in 1981 as a turning point in her life, making her realise that she could do anything if she wanted it enough. Happiness, for her, comes from stopping to think and see, valuing silence, mindfulness, compassion and, above all, following your own path.

Sonas

Celtic Thoughts on Happiness

Compiled by
Catherine Conlon

HACHETTE
BOOKS
IRELAND

First published in 2009 by Hachette Books Ireland

A Hachette UK Ltd Company

Collection © Catherine Conlon, 2009
Individual pieces © contributors, 2009
Foreword © Christina Noble, 2009

A CIP catalogue record for this title is available from the British Library.

ISBN 978 0 340 99317 0

Cover, text design by Anú Design, Tara
Printed and bound in the UK by CPI Mackays, Chatham, ME5 8TD

Hachette Books Ireland policy is to use papers that are natural, renewable and
recyclable products and made from wood grown in sustainable forests. The
logging and manufacturing processes are expected to conform to the environmental regulations of the country of origin.

Hachette Books Ireland
8 Castlecourt Centre
Castleknock
Dublin 15
Ireland

A division of Hachette UK Ltd, 338 Euston Road, London NW1 3BH, England

This book is for my children

Abby, Luke, Conor, Charlie.

That you will keep it with you through the years and
remember that these words were written for you, with love.

CONTENTS

INTRODUCTION

WHILE I CAN'T IDENTIFY THE PRECISE moment when the idea for this book occurred to me, I know that it began to take shape in my mind sometime towards the end of the summer of 2008.

The recession had not yet started, and I was increasingly conscious of feeling that, as my young children were embarking on their teenage years, we in Ireland were swimming in a sea of negativity and commercialism in which it appeared, from the outside at any rate, that happiness could only be bought with the latest gadget, outfit or handbag. Everywhere I looked, the world was full of noise and gadgetry: computers, iPods, DVDs and, of course, mobile phones. Young people especially seemed to be caught in the thrall of all this technology: groups of kids everywhere, walking along the street, all with their mobiles, staring into these technical toys.

In contrast to this overwhelming culture of consumerism, my own experience was that happiness came from valuing what I already had: family; friends; the community I lived in; long walks in the fresh air beside the sea. Also hard work, and listening to that voice inside your head reminding you of your dreams and what you wanted to achieve.

Pondering all of this, I found myself wondering: what does happiness mean in Ireland in the twenty-first century? It occurred to me that the world, even with all its current problems, is still full of beauty and challenge and hope. I suppose I felt compelled, for my own sake, but most of all, for the sake of my children and others like them, to explore the true meaning of happiness through the eyes of people I really admired. People who, in their own way, had hopes and aspirations and had gone out of their way to fulfil them and make a difference in the lives of others. In that sense, the idea for this book was born out of my own need to challenge the way that modern society seems to be heading, to show my children that life doesn't have to be like that. It doesn't have to be about stress and deadlines and pressure and noise.

As I mulled over how I would go about exploring what happiness means for Irish people, I began to make a list of the kind of people I wanted to approach. People from all walks of life, who have followed a path that has led to success in their own field and in their own terms. Not all of them are well known, but all have done something lasting and fulfilling in their lives. I decided that I would ask them about what has helped them to succeed: their motivation, philosophy and sources of challenge, happiness and joy.

Gradually, the list became longer. Every day, I would read something, hear a snippet on the radio, or somebody would tell me a story about how one person had affected them in a way that was deep and lasting. At first, I wrote letters. Ireland is a small country with a small population. It is not difficult to get a letter to someone who is reasonably well known. Gradually, I got responses: firstly, a trickle and then, day by day, a steady, even flow of replies. Soon, I was sending e-mails, too, and the response became even greater. Almost without exception, people's reactions have been heart-warming and positive. In that sense, this book is not just about the result, it has also been about the journey.

As the contributions began to come in, one piece particularly appealed to me. Paul Sreenan SC summed up happiness as including nine essential elements: Gratitude, Mindfulness, Light-Heartedness, Kindness, Understanding, Compassion, Self-Love, Freedom of Mind and Peace. This really struck a chord with me, at a time when I was trying to work out how I would pull all the one hundred or so contributions together. And so I decided to use these qualities as chapter divisions and found that all the pieces fitted more or less under one of these headings.

Something else happened to me that summer, which would also have an important influence on this book. While browsing in a second-hand bookshop in Ballinskelligs, where my family and I regularly spend our holidays, I happened to pick up Christina Noble's book, *Bridge Across my Sorrows*. I feel it is no coincidence that this inspirational memoir fell into my lap at that particular time. Given my preoccupation with the question of happiness in Ireland today, so much in the story of this amazing woman struck a chord with me. Christina is living proof that happiness and fulfilment come from compassion, love and kindness, and the drive to make a difference to the lives of others. Her conviction that it is as important to feed the heart and soul as it is to feed the body – as is evident from the emphasis in all her programmes on love and kindness and, above all, having fun – coincides very strongly with my own beliefs, and, indeed, echoes my own original purpose in putting this book together for my own children and others like them.

For these reasons, this book is dedicated to the CNCF, and all proceeds will go to this wonderful charity, which works to try to meet some of the massive needs in the developing world, where a small amount can make a huge difference to those who have nothing. Like Christina Noble, I believe that we can all help in a significant way, by being aware and having the confidence that each one of us can make a difference.

In this context, I would like to thank each and every one of the contributors here for the great generosity and goodwill they have shown in giving their time and in sharing the rich diversity of their insights and experiences in these pages.

It is my hope that the profits from this book will make a real difference, in the years to come, to the lives of children who have nothing.

That thought fills me with joy.

Catherine Conlon

FOREWORD

I LOVE LOVE, BECAUSE LOVE IS all powerful. Real love has to come from inside – a bit like a river, flowing through every blood vessel in your body, through the pit of the stomach, up into the soul and heart, and it speaks through the eyes. It is freedom. It is passion. We should not be afraid to show it, to distribute it to our fellow human beings and all living things, bringing results more powerful than any bombs – but only if it is unconditional, pure, clean love. It can make dreams come true, bring people together and give hope to children where there was none.

Love is like an adhesive that brings worlds, cultures and creeds together. The sad thing is that the word 'love' is used so loosely sometimes, to sound good. A celebrity who has just won an award may say, 'I love you all.' Or it can be used in a magazine: 'I love your dress, I love your car – wow! In fact, I love everything about you!' I guess all of this is okay, provided that when it comes down to it, the same people have the ability to show real love and understand what that is.

I really believe that the world has neglected our children. We are all citizens of planet earth and yet are shocked by some of the horrific images we see on our television screens, and in magazines and newspapers, of starving children, homeless children, children who have been trafficked into the sex industry or sold for body parts. Young children who mis-guidedly think that the one who holds the gun is God. Young people, so full of rage, who have never known love, who want to feel all-powerful, and find this power in the destruction of human life and the maiming of others. Tit-for-tat. You get me and I'll get you. Why? It's like a giant revolving wheel that is unable to stop. Then there are those who become the street pharmacists, buying and selling crack, cocaine, heroin and meths.

Who needs a bomb, when the new generation are doing it for the bomb? We are the worst terrorists to each other. We are blinded with celebrity and fashion, which change every few weeks. Magazines promoting unrealistic images, encouraging the malnourished look, endless plastic surgery and makeovers – and, whilst there is a place for all these things, with balance, there is no balance here.

I'm proud to say I have met hundreds and thousands of young people across the world who do care. Global ambassadors, who are working hard to make changes, by bringing love and hope to those who never had a chance to begin with. The very foundations of the projects I started were based on love, and the reason these projects have been successful is that the people involved, worldwide, really care and give their love unconditionally – and mean it. Long live love. But we have to act on it, otherwise nothing changes. A raging fire will not go out on its own: we have to extinguish it.

I believe that everyone, whatever their creed or religion, can work together, with the power of love. For love is the greatest weapon we humans possess.

Christina Noble

Christina Noble's story is one of bravery and resilience. After the death of her mother when she was just ten years of age, Christina and her siblings were taken into care and sent to different orphanages. As a child and teenager, she endured extreme hardship which eventually led to homelessness, and this hardship continued into adult life. Yet, despite everything, Christina found the strength to fight back and against all the odds, in 1991, she founded the Christina Noble Children's Foundation (CNCF), in Ho Chi Minh City, Vietnam, and has, to date, helped over 180,000 poor and desperate children and their families in that country. In 1997, Christina expanded operations into Mongolia. There are currently over 100 active projects in cities and provinces, ranging from the substantial Social and Medical Centre in the heart of Ho Chi Minh City, to the construction of water wells in the remote Gia Canh Village.

Christina's commitment to the welfare of children is rooted in her own experiences and she has dedicated her life to helping children throughout the world. While acknowledging that medical facilities are essential, Christina is always first to point out that fun is the foundation of life, maintaining that 'every child has the right to a childhood'. Today, hundreds of children in the foundation's care learn at schools and partake in music and sports projects.

GRATITUDE

I find that gratitude is something that often comes after the event. We will be grateful for a glorious week of sunshine, when the mists and rains return. When we are besieged with illness, we will be grateful for the health we once had.

Each of the contributors in this section recognise the value of being grateful for what we have – and what we have had – and the way in which this awareness can wonderfully enrich our everyday lives.

I find Anita Notaro's piece particularly inspiring, as she describes how, after serious illness, she developed the daily ritual of giving thanks for all the things that went right that day. Adi Roche's sheer *joie de vivre* is infectious, as is her determination to enjoy all the good things about her life. Darren Clarke's thoughts on gratitude are simple and profound, as he contemplates the legacy left to him and his family after the death of his wife, Heather.

My own experience has been that my ability to appreciate all that I have is greatly enhanced when I step back from the frenetic pace and the daily whirl of activity that is my world.

One way I do this is by going for long walks with our dog along the riverside path from Blackrock Castle to Rochestown in Cork. Much more occasionally, I take a drive down to Murroe in Co. Limerick on a Friday evening, and step into the cloistered surrounds of Glenstal Abbey for forty-eight hours. Here, I take off my jacket and breathe a sigh of relief. Silence. No phones, television or children. Surrounded only by woods and lakes and the ancient walls of the castle. No demands or deadlines. Only the invitation to tranquil prayer five times a day. Waking to the sound of the church bell at 6.30 a.m., and walking across to the church, and the gentle call to thank the Lord at the start of each day.

An opportunity to give thanks, to listen to your heart and soul.

MICK O'CONNELL

Count your blessings, and name them one by one

PEOPLE EVERYWHERE IN THIS LIFE HAVE their ups and downs: some certainly have severe trials and tribulations. But the many blessings cannot be overlooked.

Personally, I thank the Lord for many things, such as:

◆ Parents who, by example, set down good standards

◆ Now, a family of my own, and the special gift of a Downs Syndrome son

All those people who I have interacted with directly and indirectly, who have enriched my life. '*Ar scáth a chéile a mhaireann na daoine.*' We all do live in each other's shadow.

The luck to be born in a beautiful place on the edge of the Atlantic, but, most importantly, the gift to appreciate the beauty and magnificence of God's creation.

As a one-time sportsman, I still value sport as a wonderful deviation from the normal cares of life. Sport is often discussed in terms of victory and defeat, triumph and disaster – that is certainly part of it, but real sport is about pastime, recreation and fair play. 'Play and let play' was always my motto.

'It matters not who won or lost, but how you played the game.'

Mick O'Connell was born on Valentia Island, Co. Kerry. His father was a fisherman, who also worked on the family's small farm on the island. From an early age, O'Connell showed his footballing talent. He played Gaelic football with the Kerry senior inter-county team from 1956–1973, and is regarded as one of the greatest Gaelic football players of all time.

ANITA NOTARO

Recovery

WHEN YOU'RE GIVEN THE ALL-CLEAR AFTER a serious illness, it's an amazing feeling. I remember when it happened to me. As I walked away from the hospital, my treatment finished, it was 30 December and it seemed like my life was starting again along with the New Year.

Recovery affects you in different ways. First, you feel utter relief that it's over. You make plans for the first time in ages. You start to look forward to simple pleasures: things you took for granted, but which are made special again simply because you're not worried any more.

Next comes gratitude. I'd had so much support, churches throughout Ireland were almost set on fire with the number of candles that were lit for me, and many people surprised me with little kindnesses. Gratitude is a great feeling, and one we should all nourish in ourselves. Every day, if you really look, you can find something to be grateful for, as I discovered during some of my own darkest days.

Later, guilt sets in, especially when you hear about others who haven't been as lucky. My tumour was discovered early only because I'd been vigilant since two colleagues in their twenties were diagnosed with breast cancer. A two-yearly medical check became routine for me, although as the years passed I became a bit lazy, especially when I was assured that for those with no family history, breast cancer was rare enough in women under fifty. After my mam died suddenly, a thought kept coming into my head, reminding me that it was almost three years since I'd had a check-up. Incredibly, because I acted on that persistent thought (my mother prodding me as usual, perhaps?), I spent only two days in hospital, had almost no side effects, didn't need chemotherapy and was able to work throughout my treatment. Sadly, this is not always the case and you do feel guilty and wonder why one person gets a seemingly easy ride while another struggles endlessly.

Then you have to deal with paranoia. Even now, three years later, the smallest health problem makes me nervous. Eventually you have to get a perspective on life, otherwise you'd drive yourself bonkers.

I suppose, when you've been through all the emotions, the overriding feeling you're left with is that there has to be a plan for each one of us, otherwise how can we explain the random nature of life, and especially health?

One of the lessons I learned during recovery was the importance of welcoming each new day and asking for the strength to deal with whatever challenges it might bring. Also, I try and remember to give thanks at the other end of the day for all the things – some very small – that worked out well. And there's always something, if you think hard enough.

Finally, I make myself say the most difficult prayer of all, because it means putting your trust in a higher power. So the final words of my night-time ritual are always, '*Not my will, but thy will be done.*'

Anita Notaro always knew she wanted to write, but only began to take it seriously when she became a journalist and television producer with RTÉ. During her time there, she directed most of the major entertainment and current-affairs programmes, including the Eurovision Song Contest *and coverage of the 1997 general election. Anita left RTÉ in 2002 to become a writer. Her first three novels,* Back After the Break, Behind the Scenes *and* The WWW Club, *have all been published by Bantam Books. When she can't stand the isolation any more, she hangs around the cast and crew of* Fair City *(Ireland's number one television soap), where they take pity on her and let her direct a few episodes now and again!*

ADI ROCHE

SOMEONE ONCE GAVE ME A QUOTATION FROM the famous nineteenth-century, Anglo-Irish politician Edmund Burke, who said, '*Nobody made a greater mistake than he who did nothing because he could only do a little.*' I loved it immediately. It is one saying that I try to hang onto always, and indeed encourage others with too. It spurs me on and I know, especially from talking to children in schools, that it seems to be something that inspires them too. I can do something! And it matters! And I matter! It's so empowering and immediate.

I also love walking. A brisk six miles, three times a week clears my cobwebs, gets the juices flowing, and I love the embrace of nature, come rain, sleet, wind or shine. I love the sounds of birds, the blue skies, the wind in my hair.

I love the radio and music, I love to sing. I love to dance. I love life and thank God for everything!

I have been so blessed in my life, and it's an honour and a privilege for me to offer a little bit of that back to the world. I have a great sense of humour and I love a bit of craic!

It keeps me going on dark days. I have a husband, a sister and brothers who love me most of the time! I love my home, my nest!

I love the holy land of West Kerry!

I am blessed.

Adi Roche is CEO and Founder of the International Children's Charity, Chernobyl Children's Project International (CCPI). Since 1997 she has been actively campaigning for issues related to the environment, peace and justice. She was unanimously elected to stand as the People's Alliance candidate for the Irish Presidency under the leadership of the Irish Labour Party in 1997. Since 1991, the CCPI has delivered over €76 million in direct and indirect humanitarian and medical aid to thousands of children and their families in Chernobyl-affected regions.

AINE LAWLOR

I'M WRITING THIS ON A COLD, wet January day that feels as miserable and as depressing as a day can get. Not the best day to be searching for something inspirational! The news nationally and internationally is even worse than the weather: free-falling recession, job losses, pay cuts, war in the Middle East. My daughter is sick and I'm just getting over the flu.

Reasons to be cheerful, or even to get out of bed on grim days like this?

My list won't be another person's. What lifts my spirit might do nothing for yours.

But even a month as horrible as this has the Turner exhibition in the National Gallery. The golds and yellows and ochres and siennas and greys and violet blues of his water-colours shine through the dim light of this month. They are a national treasure, free to the public, only on show every January. They warm my heart and my eyes.

On Saturday, it is my grandmother's ninety-seventh birthday, and my sisters and I are going to visit her. She has buried one husband and three children, one of them my mother. She has survived serious illness and endured the kind of hard life my generation cannot imagine. And yet the wonderful part of 'Gaggy', as we all call her, is the way that she loves and lives life, is still active, always ready for the funny story, or a song or an outing. She reminds me of something I too often forget: that happiness is an attitude as much as a set of circumstances.

The first snowdrop has pushed through in the front garden. By the end of the month, there'll be little winter irises to join them. The seed and bulb catalogues for this summer arrive in the post, bringing with them hope of colour and long days and hours spent outside. I spend these dark nights imagining schemes and making lists for a nirvana that will probably be eaten by slugs and either battered by rain or parched with drought, but now, in my imagination, this January is just perfect.

Reasons to be cheerful. One, two, three.

Aine Lawlor joined RTÉ in 1984 as a trainee journalist before becoming a reporter and presenter in 1988. She has worked on the Pat Kenny Show, Today at 5, *RTÉ 2fm* News *and a variety of television programmes, including* The Nature of Things, Tuesday File *and the highly acclaimed series,* States of Fear. *She currently co-presents* Morning Ireland, *the flagship morning news programme on RTÉ Radio 1. She is married to Ian Wilson and they have four children.*

MARY O'ROURKE TD

THIS VERY CHALLENGE HAS FORCED ME to focus on my inward thinking, on what my philosophy for living is and what my motivation is.

My idea of living is very much in the lines of the Country and Western song, 'One Day at a Time, Sweet Jesus'. I am not very good at long-term planning, but I am comfortable with sorting myself out at the end of each evening about what I will be doing, saying, and where I will be going the next day. Sometimes, we dwell obviously on the past or luxuriate in hope for the future, whereas the present is far more interesting and, after all, we live in the present.

So, what motivates me to live each day to the full, doing all I possibly can encompass in my job?

My present job is very much lived at a gallop, Dublin three to four days a week, and then the rest of the time back in my constituency, and particularly back in my home in Athlone. I try to keep myself very engrossed in my work and I love my present position as a very vocal backbencher. I never had the opportunity to be that before, and I now luxuriate in speaking each week in the Dáil and as often as possible on radio, television, and so on. It certainly keeps the wheels of life, as well as me myself, oiled up!

My real source of happiness is my family, and I am so unashamedly proud of them: my two lovely sons, their gorgeous wives and their beautiful loving children. I never thought that I would gain such utter happiness from children, but I have, and now a second time. Once with my own children, when they were young, and now with my grandchildren, all five of them. They love me and I love them.

When Enda, my husband, died, I never thought I would love again, indeed, for a time, I thought I would never live again. An inner part of me will always be labelled 'Enda'. Of course, the sorrow does not lessen, but it does become less acute and less all-pervasive in my life. In a way, my grandchildren have begun to fill that void: how wonderful that is too, because of course it is human life recreating itself, bringing with it such sweet joy and such sweet sorrow too.

No matter what job in life you have, that job can be done to the full, and that is what matters: giving your all to the job in hand. Of course I was a government minister, yes, of course I was Deputy Leader of Fianna Fáil, and of course that brought excitement, highs and lows. But now my life is even more rounded – a backbench job speaking up for and working for people, a family who surround me with love and my happy, golden memories.

Pollyanna? Yes, that's me.

Mary O'Rourke has been a member of Dáil Éireann for over twenty years, during which time she held ministerial positions in Education, Health, Trade and Marketing, Labour Affairs and Public Enterprise. She was Deputy Leader of Fianna Fáil from 1995-2002, and a senator and Leader of Seanad Éireann and Spokesperson on Northern Ireland from 2002-2007. She is widowed with two sons.

Philip McDonagh

In Memory of My Mother
(Died November 15th, 1945)

Patrick Kavanagh, 1939-1946

You will have the road gate open, the
front door ajar
The kettle boiling and a table set
By the window looking out at
the sycamores –
And your loving heart lying in wait

For me coming up among
the poplar trees.
You'll know my breathing and my walk
And it will be a summer evening on
those roads,
Lonely with leaves of thought.

We will be choked with the grief of
things growing,
The silence of dark-green air

Life too rich – the nettles, docks
and thistles
All answering the prodigal's prayer.

You will know I am coming though
I send no word
For you were lover who could tell
A man's thoughts – my thoughts –
though I hid them – Through you
I knew Woman and did not fear
her spell.

Where do we turn in times of suffering and uncertainty?

In Auschwitz, Primo Levi and another prisoner recited Dante. When Anna Akhmatova composed her long poem *Requiem*, a group of friends, ten altogether, committed the work to memory: it was risky to keep the manuscript in Stalin's Russia. When Job is afflicted in the Bible, at least one of his friends tries poetry as a response.

What kind of poetry can make a difference in such circumstances? Patrick Kavanagh's poem about his mother's death has at least some of the elements that make for consolation.

♦   First, there is the paradox that the poet breaks the

oppressive silence of which he speaks by writing the poem. He brings grief into the open.

♦   Second, there is nothing of bitterness in this bereaved man walking among the poplar trees – no rage or violence, no scorn, no despair.

♦   Third, there is the sudden rise of beauty in the verse: '*By the window looking out at the sycamores . . .*'

♦   Fourth, there is the quality of the human relationship that runs through the poem. Home is a place apart. The mention of the prodigal tells us that the peace of the home is in part the peace of forgiveness. Kavanagh celebrates the particular: when life is too rich, '*nettles, docks and thistles*' answer the prodigal's prayer.

Paddy's mother's actions are described in the future tense: '*You will have the road gate open*'; '*You will know I am coming though I send no word*'. Quiet moments that mother and son have shared hold something of immortality.

So, what do we make of the poet's dream-like vision of his mother? Is the hinted-at Christian theology a means to an artistic end, the deployment of tradition to add colour to the poem? Or is the horizon of hope a part of Kavanagh, an inner reality or resource that he both loves and recognises as true?

Kavanagh offers us a clue to the answer. His use of ordinary phrases, the moments at which the quick poetic hare delib-erately becomes a tortoise, suggest a delicacy on the poet's part: beauty stepping back a little in the presence of truth and goodness.

Philip McDonagh has had a number of assignments as an official of the Department of Foreign Affairs and was appointed as Ambassador to Russia in 2009. His secondary schooling was at Gonzaga College, Dublin. He later studied Classics at Balliol College, Oxford. His volumes of poetry include Carraroe in Saxony *and* Memories of an Ionian Diplomat. *Philip is married to Ana Grenfell and they have two daughters.*

Louis Mulcahy

Perspectives

Louis Mulcahy, 2000

How lesser things divert us from what should
fascinate us.
How conditions of the climate fix our course.
How a radiating beam, waving from a light-
house, may be a beacon of disaster if ignored.

How Plasmacytoma, in face of Multiple
Myeloma, brought relief. How radiation
through the haze burned away the horror that
tore from rusty anchors concern so long
submerged beneath the surging waves.

*Louis Mulcahy is a potter who with his wife, Lisbeth, set up
Potadoireacht na Caloige on the Dingle Peninsula. He was recently awarded an Honorary Doctorate by the National University of
Ireland in recognition of his artistry and his contribution to the
economic and cultural welfare of his Gaeltacht community.*

DARREN CLARKE

THE FOLLOWING IS A QUOTATION WHICH is engraved on the headstone of my wife, Heather. It's from the late Dana Reeve, wife of Christopher, and has given me strength through some pretty tough times:

> 'Don't be sad for what you've lost.
> Smile for what you've had.'

Northern Ireland's Darren Clarke has been a European Tour professional golfer since 1990. He has won a total of eighteen events worldwide and has represented Europe in five Ryder cups. Darren lost his wife, Heather, to cancer in August 2006, and is a great supporter of breast cancer charities. He arranges his golfing schedule around their two sons, Tyrone and Conor.

FINBAR WRIGHT

CARVED INTO A BLOCK OF STONE, embedded in the rockery behind the small nun's convent at the side of Farranferris College, is the dictat: '*Ní airimid ach na laethanta (gréine)*'. ('We count only the sunny days'). Some cleric with a wry sense of humour may have put it there to alleviate the despondency often associated with the lousy diet and harsh regimes of a boarding school.

As a student there in the mid-1970s and as a teacher there in the 1980s, I often admired the old Gaelic script chiselled on that stone and, of all the wonderful knowledge that I must surely have soaked up within the walls of that school, the wisdom of that phrase has remained fixed deeply in my mind as an abiding philosophy. Just as the earth and nature draw life from the sun, our body, spirit and soul will not thrive without some ray of happiness or at least a memory of happiness, however flimsy or tenuous it may be.

Remembering a happy place or time or event has cleverly and traditionally been used to good effect throughout history by those who find themselves in impossible situations of misery and terror. Happy memories caress the soul and help us rise above the mental and physical cruelties of the world. I am lucky in my career, in that music is closely associated with special moments in people's lives, and the sparking and rekindling of memories is a privilege which I deeply appreciate. I can feel the hearts of an audience rise and swell when I sing, 'We'll build a bonfire of our troubles and watch them blaze away', for there in the flames they see the reflection of the sun, and they answer the command of that old Irish phrase, 'We count only the sunny days'.

International musician, Finbar Wright, was born in Kinsale, County Cork, and studied in Palencia, Spain, Maynooth University and University College Cork. He began his professional music career in 1990. Since then, Finbar has recorded numerous albums, presented regular programmes on television and toured the world as a performer. He has entertained many notable figures, including Pope John Paul II, and Presidents Ronald Reagan and Bill Clinton. He has performed with Jerry Lee Lewis, Montserrat Caballé, Kiri Te Kanawa, and celebrated composer Andrew Lloyd Webber. Hilary Clinton, US Secretary of State, recently described Finbar as, 'one of Ireland's most affable, illustrious and loved ambassadors of music'.

Peter Flanagan

A FEW DAYS AGO, in the run-up to Christmas, Isabelle, my 12-year-old, asked me, 'Daddy, is Santa affected by the recession?'

My immediate thought was to say, 'Of course he is', and to lower her expectations – but then, how could he be? How could the magic be affected by the mundane? Isn't the transcendent supposed to transcend the material?

If it does not, then how are we to attempt to maintain our happiness and peace in the face of buffeting change? Is it simply a state of mind, as for Milton's Satan in *Paradise Lost*, who says: *'The mind is its own place and in it self/Can make a Heav'n of Hell, a Hell of Heav'n . . .'?'*

Or is there any objective trail or evidence towards sourcing happiness?

It seems to me that there are many examples over the last 2000 years, and indeed now, of people who have managed to find this peace, or who are on this journey of discovery. It is worth looking at some of their shared characteristics.

They have a childlike simplicity, live in the present and avoid torturing themselves with the fear of uncertain futures. They are interested in everything and everyone as unique. They are eager to trust, to seek out the good with enthusiasm, to learn until they draw their last breath and to grow in the love of others. They know that they are happiest when focused on other people's needs rather than their own, and that self-absorption is a sure recipe for misery.

Other characteristics of such people are that they develop what has been called a notion of otherness: recognition of their own weakness and of pain in the world, and of the gulf that exists between perfection and human shortcomings. They have a belief outside of themselves in a loving creator who cares about them uniquely, and they have a hunger to develop this relationship. This is the beginning of prayer. St Thérèse of Lisieux, ('the Little Flower'), described it beautifully when she wrote: '*For me, prayer is a surge of the heart; it is a simple look turned towards Heaven, it is a cry of recognition and of love, embracing both trial and joy.*' The joy of hope springs from this. We know that whatever trials come, they will pass and that they will have served some purpose.

The people I am talking of also experience a sense of loving duty and a desire to inform their growing conscience. They are happiest when doing their jobs well, especially when the going gets tough. In *The Lord of the Rings*, when Frodo is tired of his mission, he cries in despair: '*I wish the ring had never come to me. I wish none of this had happened.*' Gandalf replies: '*So do all who live to see such things. But that is not for them to decide. All we have to decide is what to do with the time that is given to us.'*

Other curious traits of these 'happy people' include self-denial and the offering up of work and suffering. Christ's Sermon on the Mount, in Chapter 5 of the Book of Matthew, sets out this radical, paradoxical path to happiness for, *'the poor in spirit, those who mourn, the meek, those who hunger and thirst after righteousness, the merciful, the pure of heart, the peacemakers and those persecuted for seeking righteousness'*. These are not different people being offered different things, but rather the different attributes of someone trying to live life in a particular way – like a saint. The kingdom of heaven, comfort, inheritance of the earth, satisfaction, mercy obtained, to see God, and the Sonship of God: these are not just offered as rewards in heaven, but as joys on earth also.

We can usefully picture those saints that we know, those that we don't, and those in progress as having a youthful sparkle of joy in their eyes as they seem to say with Pope John Paul II: *'Do not be afraid … We are loved.'*

As Shakespeare (or, by the grace of God, St William!) proclaims in his sonnet: *'Then happy I that love and am beloved/Where I may not remove, nor be removed.'*

Peter Flanagan was born in Buncrana, Co. Donegal. Exiled to Dublin for over twenty-five years now, he is father to four wonderful children. Happy selling furniture to optimistic customers, he is constantly humbled by the love of family and friends there and here.

MINDFULNESS

S O MANY THOUGHTS GO THROUGH MY head under this heading. I look out of my window and see the starlings picking at the gravel on this cold, clear day in early February. Clear skies at last, after the horrendous mist and drizzle of the past two weeks. I battle with competing desires: the need to write some of these thoughts down, and the urge to grab coat, scarf and dog and head out into the sunshine to feel the wind in my hair and the salt off the sea on my skin.

I am mindful of the health of my children, the solid support of my husband and the all-encompassing joy of my family, even when they are all driving me crazy! I am mindful of the art of happiness, where I learn to hold my tongue and to react with patience and reason. I am mindful of the millions of young children in the world who do not have a meal, a home, a family or a future. I am mindful enough of all this to want to do something about it, and to remember that this is not charity, but justice. I am conscious of the need to react and keep reacting, and to teach my children that the future of so many is in their hands.

Once again, I find that silence is invaluable in reaching that meditative state where true mindfulness becomes possible. The truth is that very often we are so surrounded by noise and bustle, that we are closed to hearing the messages that are coming to us and the answers that we seek.

For me, this state of oneness with the world can be found in certain places too. The area around Ballinskelligs, for example, is my favourite place in the whole world. We have a cottage there, where we spend as much time as we can during the summer and on Bank Holidays. Days are spent walking, cycling, fishing, jumping off the pier, climbing Coonanna Mountain and surfing in St Finian's Bay. Some evenings, we take a run over to Portmagee and have dinner in the pub, while the sun sets over Valentia Island. It is wonderful, unspoilt. To feel the sun on your bones and the wind in your hair. To wear the same pair of shorts for two weeks and not even notice. Where there is time to think and laugh and play and listen to the sound of the ocean. A place where you can feel and hear and sense the glory of God and be at one with the world, and which always makes me think of John O'Donohue's evocative lines in *Divine Beauty: The Invisible Embrace*: *'God is breath-near, skin-touch, mind-home, heart-nest, thought-forest, otherness-river, night-well, time-salt, moon-wings, soul-fold . . .'*

For me, there is the same feel to many of the contributions in the pages that follow. The sheer, simple beauty of Liam Lawton's description of the Swedish landscape on the way to Skinnskatteberg; Jane Powers' compelling sense of *'being part of this huge and magnificent continuum'*; Ivan Perry's wonderful evocation of *'the mystical embedded in the ordinary'*: all of these convey the sense in which happiness lies in remembering that, as Liam Lawton expresses it so beautifully, we are part of the *'divine and eternal canvas, flawed and all [as we are]'*.

Liam Lawton

Between Worlds

Ahmad Shamlu

At night
When the silver moonstream
Makes a lake of limitless plain
I spread the sails of my thoughts
In the path of the wind ...

I am travelling through the centre of Sweden, on my way to Skinnskatteberg. It is nightfall and yet it is bright. Across the plain, the night dew rises to the edge of the forest.

Sweden is the country of the lupen. Graceful and tall, these wildflowers grow along the roadsides and field corners. Purple, magenta and royal blue, they rise like trumpets in a song of praise to their Creator. Here and there, red wooden barns dot the landscape, silhouetted against a crimson sky. It is well into the night and yet the northern skies are bright with light.

It seems as if the day does not want to lie down. It draws every last breath out of the hours.

Kalle, my driver, points to the lake. A wooden boat drifts slowly while a young couple lie facing the stars. There is an ease on the water. A wild bird, who has not yet given in to sleep, soars and swoops, looking for the last catch. Across the lake, the shadow of a church steeple skirts the water, reaching into the heavens. The white-washed walls are hidden beneath the cover of woodland. In the distance, the pine forest waits for the oncoming night and all its creatures prepare for a night dance.

Like a painter in motion, I freeze-frame the memory, never knowing when I will need this image again. There is nothing as beautiful as a Nordic dusk, where day and night are suspended, and mere humans are left dangling between two worlds.

In the twilight, I take leave of the day. Now time is suspended and there is nothing I can do but be still. In the city I have just left, there is no time to be still or silent. It is frantically busy. Here, however, I am confronted by stillness itself. Here, the only music I hear is the music of silence, and it is beautiful.

Before me, the lake appears like a sheet of soft glass. It mirrors my thoughts to me. I cannot turn away. So often, we run from such moments, when life affords us time to ponder and God whispers in our ear. But we do not know how to listen and we do not want to hear.

The light is dying, but I do not feel alone. Something within tells me that I am not alone. I am in the presence of divine beauty, in the presence of God, the Creator of all that is good and beautiful. All I need to do now is simply to be.

As the night breeze blows softly, the words of the ancient psalmist come to me: '*You search me, God, and you know me.*' Here I can acknowledge the dark and light of my own life. The vulnerable and the strong can dwell side by side without pretence or mask. The beauty of this place allows the soul to be tranquil and honest. At times I sigh deeply, remembering the harsh realities of life's encounters, and at times I smile, as memory reminds me of other blessings and other souls that have enlightened my own pathway. In the beautiful mind of God, at this very moment, I become part of His divine and eternal canvas, flawed as I am. He calls me here. It is not by coincidence. It is the gift of His giving. I may be incomplete, imperfect, flawed and weak, but I am straining towards my own perfection to become one with God, who will never cease drawing us to Himself.

The wind kisses my face and the water laps the wooden boat. The night dew creeps over the surface and the lonesome birdsong becomes a distant cry. All is caught up in the mystery and awesome beauty of this moment. If only the world learned to stop and listen.

Soon it will be morning and the sun will rise over Skinnskatteberg. Night will nestle behind the wooden shed where lake reeds sway in silent reverence, and God will hide among the lupens.

Liam Lawton is a multiplatinum composer who specialises in sacred and spiritual music. He has performed in many countries and has released a number of albums. Originally from Edenderry in Co. Offaly, Liam now resides in Carlow and is a Roman Catholic priest.

Tom Arnold

Digging

from *Death of a Naturalist* by
Seamus Heaney, 1966

Between my finger and my thumb
The squat pen rests; snug as a gun.

Under my window, a clean rasping sound
When the spade sinks into gravelly ground:
My father, digging. I look down

Till his straining rump among
the flowerbeds
Bends low, comes up twenty years away
Stooping in rhythm through potato drills
Where he was digging.

The coarse boot nestled on the lug, the shaft
Against the inside knee was levered firmly.
He rooted out tall tops, buried the
bright edge deep
To scatter new potatoes that we picked,
Loving their cool hardness in our hands.

By God, the old man could handle a spade.
Just like his old man.

My grandfather cut more turf in a day
Than any other man on Toner's bog.
Once I carried him milk in a bottle
Corked sloppily with paper.
He straightened up
To drink it, then fell to right away
Nicking and slicing neatly, heaving sods
Over his shoulder, going down and down
For the good turf. Digging.

The cold smell of potato mould, the squelch
and slap
Of soggy peat, the curt cuts of an edge
Through living roots awaken in my head.
But I've no spade to follow men like them.

Between my finger and my thumb
The squat pen rests.
I'll dig with it.

I have an enormous regard for Seamus Heaney as a writer
and a human being. More than forty years on, 'Digging',
his first poem in his first collection, *Death of a Naturalist*,
combines his gifts for words and observation with a declara-
tion of commitment to his chosen art. That commitment has

been delivered on with constancy and enriched by great scholarship. Heaney uses words, in his poems and his every-day speech, with such care and precision. And he combines these gifts with a natural grace and modesty which is very special.

Tom Arnold was appointed Chief Executive of Concern Worldwide, Ireland's largest humanitarian organisation, in 2001. He was previously Assistant Secretary General with the Irish Department of Agriculture and Food. He also worked for the European Commission for ten years.

Jane Powers

When I was a child, one of my least favourite Catholic rituals was when, on Ash Wednesday, the priest took his big, gritty thumb and smeared ash on my forehead, saying: 'Dust thou art, and unto dust shalt thou return.' It made me squirm with unworthiness: I was a grubby child being punished for sins unknown, and being made grubbier by this stern and unforgiving man in a swaying white dress.

If only I had known then what I know now, I might have been comforted, instead of discomfited. The 'dust' that I was being called was not the grey, dead stuff that lay under the pews and kneelers in the cold church. It was, in fact, soil – the life-giver and the life-receiver, the material that sup ported the immeasurable numbers of plants and animals that went before me, and that would continue to do the same for all that came after. My life came from the soil, and in my death I would return to it, to nourish further life.

I was – indeed, I am – just one tiny particle of the seething mass of life on this planet: all the birds of the air; all the animals; all the insects, worms and other invertebrates of the land; all the fish of the sea; all the plants; all the people.

I didn't tie all this together until I had been gardening for some years: sowing and growing, composting, and helping to make new life out of old. It's something that every gardener feels sooner or later. And, for me now, the idea of being part of this huge and magnificent continuum is deeply satisfying. It is both exhilarating and levelling to sit still for a minute at the end of the garden, while all around me plants and creatures are cycling through their lives, some fast, some slow – but all part of the greatest chemical and physical process in the world. Life itself. I am of the earth, and it is of me.

Jane Powers is a garden writer and photographer. She contributes a weekly column to The Irish Times.

SHEILA O'FLANAGAN

That the birds of worry and care fly above your head, this you cannot change.
But that they make nests in your hair, this you can prevent.

Chinese Proverb

I GET STRESSED VERY EASILY BECAUSE I'm a perfectionist (or, as my friends call me, a control freak). Anything I do, I like to do to the best of my ability, and I expect other people to have the same attitude. But not everybody does. Some people are happy just to get a job done. I get frustrated by this in the same way as I get frustrated about major global issues and the fact that many of our political leaders seem to have based their philosophy on the pigs in Orwell's *Animal Farm*.

But you can't take the weight of the world on your shoulders and you can't have everything exactly the way you want it. It has taken me a long time to realise this, and a long time to accept it. The proverb above helps me whenever I'm getting tense about a situation over which I have no control. I know that I'm right to be concerned but I might not always have the answer.

Wanting to do my best is what motivates me, but actually I'm happiest outdoors, in warm weather, gazing up at the sky. I love knowing that as night falls, the stars will appear and that I'm looking at the same stars as everyone who lived before me and those who will come after. It's a great way of putting things into perspective and of realising that what I might consider to be enormous problems are nothing but specks in space and time.

Sheila O'Flanagan is a bestselling author whose novels have been translated into twenty-two languages. Prior to writing full-time, Sheila pursued a very successful career in banking and finance. She writes a regular business column for The Irish Times *and in her spare time plays competitive badminton.*

Nóirín Ní Ríain

Listen that you may live ...
from *The Book of Isaiah*

WHEN YOU LISTEN TO THE SOUND of your own beautiful voice, you open your heart to another dimension. Heart-work is ear-work: heart is simply the word 'ear' embraced and cradled by an 'h' and a 't'.

'*Listen, with the ear of the heart*', was the very first intimate counsel given to us by St Benedict over 1,500 years ago, and one which promises a holy, nourishing life. All your fears collapse and disappear as you allow yourself to be moved by what you hear.

There is a direct line from your throat, your larynx, to the inner ear which, in turn, runs on to the brain. As a result, bodily sounds do not have to leave your body to be heard. Every vocal sound - spoken, cried, laughed, sighed, shouted, whispered - is heard first only by you in your own ear. Your larynx cannot keep secrets from your ear. The voice and the ear are one: they are simply two sides of the one coin. No other person can hear precisely these glorious head sounds.

After the human voice leaves the body to communicate to the world around, its sound changes. We sometimes cringe at the spoken message snippet on our phones, 'Surely that's not me!' And it isn't! After sound leaves the perfect tuning of the body, it's off-key. No other being hears your true voice, the passport to your soul. For thousands of years, the sound of your voice has been sculpted and refined. You have no idea how carefully your own voice has been fine-tuned, long before you were born, in the womb. *Truly you have formed my inmost being; you knit me in my mother's womb. I give you thanks that I am wonderfully made ... My soul also you knew full well.* (Psalm 139)

Only you (and your Creator, who is always listening) can vaguely hear the echo of your soul or imagine its full capacity. This is 'theosony' (from the Greek *theos*, meaning God, and the Latin *sonans*, meaning sounding): the natural, stunning, wholesome sound of God.

Nóirín Ní Ríain is an internationally acclaimed spiritual singer who has recorded several CDs and is also an author of books and articles. A theologian and musicologist, Nóirín was awarded the first ever Doctorate in Theology from Mary Immaculate College, University of Limerick, in 2003. Her thesis subject was Towards a Theology of Listening, *for which she coined the new term, 'theosony'.*

Maxi

Value

THAT'S THE KEYWORD. THAT WORD IS the Map, the Dictionary, the Thesaurus, the Recipe and the Wand. The 'value' word is the Healing Ointment to our open scars and sores.

He left you because he didn't value you any more.

He spent so much because he felt undervalued.

She didn't attend because she found what she thought was a more valuable way to spend her time.

She got his attention by speaking to him about something he valued.

She didn't value the control of her own life. She gave it to someone else whose only value on it was to enhance theirs. Eventually they got bored. To feel the power they once felt when they made decisions on her behalf, they slowly drained her life of anything she valued, and left her too stunned to do anything but ask for more of the same, in the hope that the feeling of value would come back. But it never will until she uncovers it within herself.

How did he get her to do that? He wrapped the bad deed in a sweet paper of disguise which advertised something she valued.

How can you get strong? Value yourself.

How can you have quality in your life? Cull the selfish. When you have, make a decision to recognise them and stop them from getting near you. If they are already near you, stop them today. No need to tell them - they won't hear you, and will move on to someone else who doesn't value themselves.

Magic. You are left with the good, truthful, nutritious, kind, caring, funny and special in this, your new, valuable life.

You value them,
They value you,
You value you –
Easy.

Maxi has been in public life for many decades. She was part of the three-girl group, Maxi, Dick and Twink, which had hit records in Ireland and toured extensively in Canada and the USA and she has represented Ireland twice in the Eurovision Song Contest. In the late 1970s, she became a member of the all-girl group, Sheeba, working on Thames Television in the UK. As a UNICEF representative, she has travelled throughout Zambia, promoting awareness of malaria. She currently presents Risin' Time, *on RTÉ Radio 1.*

Mary Kennedy

Last night as I was sleeping,
I dreamt – marvellous error! –
that I had a beehive
here inside my heart.
And the golden bees
were making white combs
and sweet honey
from my old failures.

from *Last Night as I Was Sleeping* by
Antonio Machado, 1903

I am constantly amazed by the power of inspirational writings to lift my mood and keep me focused and positive. We all have our good days and our down days and when things are looking a bit bleak a few lines like those above, from the Spanish poet Antonio Machado can really lift my mood. We all make mistakes, we all know success and failure and isn't it a nice idea that while we're sleeping the bees are busy turning our mistakes into sweet honey?

Another quotation I like is from the pen of Emma Goldman, a major figure in the history of American feminism, which goes like this: '*I'd rather have roses on my table than diamonds on my neck.*'

I love gardening, so I agree wholeheartedly with that statement. Flowers of all kinds make me happy and put a smile on my face and I always like to have fresh flowers around the house. Yet I think there's a deeper meaning here too which is worth noting. There is so much emphasis put on wealth, materialism and consumer goods that we're in danger of losing sight of the real feelings of wellbeing we can get from the simple things in life. Keeping up with the demands of consumerism can be a relentless and empty struggle, whereas the non-commercial aspects of life are much more likely to satisfy and genuinely make us happy.

Mary Kennedy is a broadcaster with RTÉ. She has worked on a variety of programmes, including Open House, *the* Eurovision Song Contest *and* Up for the Match. *She currently presents* Nationwide *on RTÉ One. Mary is the author of two books,* Paper Tigers *and* Lines I Love.

IVAN PERRY

Overworked Words

I ENJOY WRITING, AND IN MY professional life I particularly enjoy writing abstracts for scientific papers. The purpose of a scientific abstract is to distil, in less than 300 words, the purpose, methods and findings from work that may have taken three to five years to complete. I am fond of saying to our students, 'You can cover a lot of ground in 300 words. Just make sure that each sentence works hard and pulls its weight by carrying relevant detail.'

This, however, is a very different assignment: a short contribution on my philosophy for living, my motivation and my sources of happiness and joy. What could be short enough or long enough to reflect on happiness, or indeed on joy, which I understand as happiness that does not depend on what happens?

Sources of joy are both personal and universal in a way that stretches tired and overworked words. Joy spills out from a space beyond words, concepts and language. A transcendent space that we glimpse in the smile of someone we love, in the shining eyes of children or in the winning try at the corner in the last minute of the game.

In Marilynne Robinson's novel, *Gilead*, the Reverend John Ames, an ageing pastor with a terminal illness, is writing to his seven-year-old son, trying to evoke a world that for him, is suffused with beauty, joy and transcendence. He says at one point: '*I really can't tell what's beautiful anymore*', and he describes the joy of blessing and baptising people, not in a spirit of superstition or legalism, but in the sense of allowing the transcendent love and joy of God to flow through him to others.

In *Divine Beauty*, John O'Donohue writes of beauty as being '*so quietly woven through our ordinary days that we hardly notice it*'. Patrick Kavanagh, in 'A Christmas Childhood', refers to '*the light between the ricks of hay and straw*' as '*a hole in Heaven's gable*'.

The poets and mystics of all traditions alert us to the mystical embedded in the ordinary, or perhaps the ordinary embedded in the mystical, the sense that there is no separate dwelling place for God. This echoes the Gospel passage where we are advised to: '*stay awake because you do not know either the day or the hour*' when the Son of Man will appear.

As a child, sitting bored and restless through Sunday mass – like our own children now, but in an era imbued with medieval theology – this injunction to stay awake was not entirely welcome. Now, it is for me a source of joy and hope, a challenge to simply wake up or, as Buddhists would put it, to engage as best I can, with the world as it is and myself as I am, with an open and gentle heart.

Ivan Perry is Professor of Public Health and Head of the Department of Epidemiology and Public Health at University College Cork. He was born in Sligo. He is married to Dr Mary Cahill and they have three children.

Rosita Boland

THE OCEAN IS WHAT PUTS EVERYTHING in perspective for me, the one thing I can always be sure of being there, in more or less the same place as when I last saw it.

When I was a child, the ocean stole my rubber flip-flops and returned instead shells, empty crabs, opaque green and smoky-grey pieces of weathered glass. In summer, I fell asleep to the consistently inconsistent sound of the waves as they snagged on rocks before they reached the beach not far from our house.

One of my clearest memories as a child at the beach is of watching an exceptionally tall man walking into the water until he literally disappeared, the horizontal horizon remaining the same, the man going on some strange, hidden, inwards journey beneath it. Until then, I had assumed the ocean was flat and shallow. I thought of the biggest object in the world I was then familiar with - an elephant - and asked my mother if an elephant would drown in the ocean, confident of what her answer would be. When she answered yes, I was stunned. The ocean could swallow an elephant? After this, I approached the water's edge with caution for some time, peering into the shallows as if expecting a cliff edge to appear darkly underneath, just a footstep away.

The ocean is always there still, putting things in perspective for me. I need to see it regularly: I get twitchy when land-locked for too long. I need to walk its littoral zone, the place that belongs to nobody, and let whatever is bothering me be measured by the expanse and mysterious underside of the ocean. After a while, the things that bother me return with their edges taken off: blunted like pieces of sea-washed glass, transformed.

Rosita Boland is a Nieman Fellow 2009 at Harvard University, and a features writer for The Irish Times.

DOMINI KEMP

A GOOD FRIEND OF MINE GAVE me a copy of *Mrs Beeton's Cookery Book*. It is one of those typically old-fashioned cookbooks and may seem out of place with regards to a woman's role in society nowadays, but it is full of incredibly wise words that are both nostalgic and true. There is one particular sentence that I am very fond of and I love to think of it as a real endorsement for good food and the impact that it has on us all, wherever we are: '*It may be said that while statesmen may carve nations, good cooks alone can consolidate them.*'

It's lovely to think that something very simple, like sitting down and eating around a table, can bring us together like nothing else. It is a reminder that in a frantic world, where the pace can be overwhelming, it is important to slow down and celebrate what you have. It's a nice maxim, as it reminds us that even the smallest contribution can be very powerful.

Domini Kemp and her sister, Peaches, own the itsagourmetbagel shops, the restaurants itsa4 and Table, and the catering company, FeastCatering & Events. Domini is also Food Writer for The Irish Times and a member of the Feast Council.

Darina Allen

FOUR GENERATIONS OF THE ALLEN FAMILY live within ten minutes of each other. It is our greatest joy to have our children and grandchildren living and working close by. Many, though not all, are involved in Ballymaloe related enterprises, whether that be food, hospitality, farming, furniture making, product development, farm, craft and kitchen shops. The ethos is always the same: grow or source the best possible produce, and treat it simply, so that it tastes delicious and nourishes, rather than merely fuelling.

At the cookery school, we have a passion for passing on cooking and gardening skills, and operate a Slow Food educational project to teach local children to cook, sow seeds and garden. The aim is to develop the organic farm around the Ballymaloe Cookery School into a living educational farm in order to teach children how the food they eat is produced and where it comes from.

We feel strongly about the importance of sourcing locally whenever possible, since it supports our own community and generates goodwill. Our growing Farmers' Market Movement is a vital part of this vision. I also believe in the value and joy of sitting down around the kitchen table with family and friends.

There are many people in the countryside with an entrepreneurial spirit. It is more vital than ever in this economic climate that the regulations they are required to comply with are proportionate to the risks involved, and that the cost of compliance is not beyond the capacity of such businesses to pay.

I seem to have inherited high energy levels, as well as a positive attitude to life. I feel much blessed to be surrounded by my supportive and loving family and friends – this is the source of my strength and motivation in life.

Darina Allen runs the internationally renowned Ballymaloe Cookery School at Shanagarry, Co. Cork. She is Ireland's most famous cook and a bestselling author who has presented eight series of television cookery programmes. She has been instrumental in setting up the Farmers' Market Movement in Ireland, is a member of the Consultation Council of the Food Safety Authority of Ireland (FSAI) and is heavily involved in the International Slow Food Movement. She is Chair of the Artisan Food Forum, and is vehemently opposed to the growing of GM crops in Ireland.

ANN HENNING JOCELYN

Nature as Art

Ann Henning Jocelyn, 2008

The other day I went to a lot of trouble,
putting flowers in a vase.
Somewhere in the recesses of my mind
I had a clear picture of what I wanted
to achieve,
and I didn't give in
until I saw it materialize before me.

'What a lovely flower arrangement!'
exclaimed a friend when she saw it,
'It looks just like one of those
seventeenth-century still lifes.'

Only then did I realise that exactly
such a painting
had been the image I'd sought so hard
to recreate.

It amused me to think that the aim of
the seventeenth-century artist
had been the very opposite –
to create a work of art that
resembled nature.
Even so, we had both been driven by
the same ambition:
to present flowers at their best.

Nature imitating art, art
imitating nature.
Put together, they represent
the best possible view of the world –
a vision no less real, no more false
than any other,
but rife with beauty, harmony and
significance.

It's there, all around us,
to be enjoyed every single day we
experience.
It costs nothing, and requires little
in the way of talents or resources.

Why then do we so often turn our
back on it?
Settle for the insipid, trivial version of
life on earth?

Is it simply because we can't be
bothered to bring out the best in the
things that surround us?
In the people we come across?
Or even in ourselves?

*Swedish-born Ann Henning Jocelyn has lived in Connemara for
many years. She is the author of the Connemara Whirlwind Trilogy,
and her contributions to the RTÉ programme A Living Word published as Keylines and Keylines for Living have appeared in many languages, including Chinese.*

ALICE TAYLOR

A Winter Blessing

MY BEST CHRISTMAS PRESENT THIS YEAR was a trailer load of timber blocks.

This took me back through the decades to the Ireland in which I grew up, where nobody bought Christmas presents because there was no surplus cash floating around. But gifts were still exchanged. My mother reared and fattened geese for the Christmas market, and some were held back and given to town and city aunts and cousins. They, in return, gave us cakes, puddings and one cousin, who had a pub, sent a timber crate of sparkling glass bottles of amber lemonade. Another with a grocery shop sent us a bulging barnbrack, and local shops where we had dealt during the year handed out boxes of biscuits or an iced cake. My father gave a favourite cousin a bag of his best Golden Wonders. During the summer, he had gone to the bog, and, if he liked you, a bag of my father's turf came your way.

In winter, some old trees came down in storms and were cut up with a cross-cut saw and then split with iron wedges into

fire-friendly-sized blocks. Neighbours too old for such stren-
uous activity got a bag of them. We were sent to get my
grandmother ready for Christmas, which meant washing her
kitchen floor, brushing her yard and then collecting holly to
decorate her house. A neighbour too old to make it to town
for messages or to the wood for holly became our responsibility. We were my mother's neighbourhood care team!

That was another world and another kind of Ireland. But this
year, a load of timber blocks brought it all back. One of my
neighbours had to take down some old fir trees, to widen his
farm entrance to facilitate modern machinery. The old trees
had for many years stood sentinel around his gateway and,
when felled, looked like fallen warriors after a battle. But these
soldiers were destined for another mission. A few weeks later,
oozing fresh sap, they charged in my back gate, cascaded out
of a high trailer and took up position outside my back door.
They still wore the remnants of their previous grey uniforms
but now their undergarments of cream and white flashed from
beneath their coats. Until their arrival, the backyard was a
winter scene of sleeping flower tubs and denuded trees. But
the fresh logs brought a sense of warmth and promise to this
bleak scene and even before they began their next campaign,
they were sending out positive signals. A load of blocks tell
many stories. They tell of the wisdom of the one who planted and of the dedicated labour of the one who saws and splits.
They are also a promise of warm fires on winter nights.

A few days later, my neighbour's young son came and stacked
the logs in a tiered reek beside the gable end of the back

porch. His grandfather had planted those trees, his father had cut them into logs and now this young lad stacked them neatly together. The trees connected three generations. Each time I went out the back door, those logs gave me a feel of good glow. They were warming my heart before they ever reached the fire. But in order to achieve their full potential, they needed the union of a good companion. Nothing lights up the heart of a log like a sod of black turf. They both come from the belly of the earth and they belong together.

Before Christmas, a Kerryman arrived into the village with a lorry load of black turf. But this turf, unlike the turf of my childhood, which was stacked in reeks, was packed in farmer's bags and stored in the backyard of a local shop. I brought in a bag and piled the turf into my old wicker basket and, beside it, stacked the logs. Together, they had the makings of a warm Christmas. When the logs and sods stand together in the fire grate, a slow love affair begins. At first, the flames lick hesitantly between them but then, as they warm to each other, sparks fly and then they blend together and begin a slow waltz. They gradually melt together to create a golden glow.

Maybe I appreciate a real fire so much because I came within a hair's breadth of not having one. Some years ago, when we were restoring our old house, the decision concerning a real fire, as opposed to clean and effortless electric, came up for discussion. Because democracy does not lead to fast decision-making, the argument meandered on. It was finally brought to a speedy conclusion when our then seven-year-old daughter announced, 'I have never lived in a house with a real fire.'

How could I, who had been reared in the shadow of the bogs, deprive my only daughter of this? Deprivation can wear many faces! Then, an old lady who lived next door to me told me: 'Alice, my dear, it would bore you to tears to watch the same little electric flame popping up and down with monotonous regularity the whole night.'

The decision was fast-forwarded, and a real fire was the unanimous conclusion. The fire became the focal point of the 'seomra ciúin' – a room where television, phone and computer are outlawed. This is a room for reading, talking or just simply looking into the fire. A real fire is as good as sitting with an old friend. It calms your spirits and soothes deep wounds. The best piece of advice I got after a sudden death in the family was to light the fire every day, and take time to simply sit in the heat and silence. It is a poultice to deep wounds. When a friend visits, tea from a nicely laid tray is also solace to the soul.

Dogs love to lie in front of a fire. As soon as our two come in the back door, they make a beeline for the 'seomra ciúin' to check if the fire is lighting. There they stretch out in ecstasy. Because they are two large dogs who do not believe in human rights, I sometimes have to jockey for space. One thing alone causes them alarm. When the logs begin to crackle and spark, they make a hasty retreat from what they regard as artillery fire. But once the solid sods of turf have calmed the exuberant logs and the meltdown begins, the dogs, with canine perception, know that it is safe to come closer.

Christmas presents take many forms, but a load of blocks is hard to beat. They warm up your Christmas and light your way into the New Year.

Alice Taylor has written many books on country living, including The Parish, *and two books of poetry. Her latest publication is* The Journey, *a complete collection of her poetry.*

Sr Stanislaus Kennedy

Mystery

from *Stillness Through my Prayers* by
Sr Stanislaus Kennedy, 2009

God of my heart,
create in me an awareness of the
impermanence, transitoriness and
limitations of the material world.
Create in me an awareness
of the permanence, endurance,
timeliness of what is spiritual, eternal.

Help me on the journey of learning
and discovering.
Teach me not to fear uncertainty and
vulnerability.
Lead me to discover inner strength,
peace, energy, joy.

The more I bless, the more I am
blessed.

Blessings never run out.
They are drawn from a bottomless
source, replenished eternally.

Sr Stanislaus Kennedy is an Irish Sister of Charity and the founder of Focus Ireland, the Inaugural Council of Young Social Innovation, Ireland and the Sanctuary. She has been instrumental in developing social service programmes that have benefited thousands of needy people throughout Ireland and Europe. For this work, she has received many awards, including Honorary Degrees of Law from Trinity College Dublin, the National University of Ireland and the Open University, as well as a presidential medal from New York University. She is the author of three bestselling books, Now is the Time, Gardening the Soul *and* Seasons of the Day.

LIGHT-HEARTEDNESS

OF ALL THE QUALITIES THAT INSPIRE happiness, this – light-heartedness – is probably the one that I find the most difficult. I tend to take things seriously. Also, like many mothers perhaps, I tend to be the one that exercises caution, the one to whom everyone says, 'Aww, Mum, you never let us have any fun.'

When we are on holiday in Kerry, a favourite occupation of my kids and my husband, Ray, is to don wetsuits, swim out to an island just off the coast and clamber over the rocks there to the old pier. Once there, they might spend hours jumping, running and diving off the pier, or checking a lobster pot that they have hung there, for crabs and once, famously, a giant lobster.

Initially, I was in absolute terror of these trips. I would spend most of the time saying things like, 'Walk, don't run!' or 'Get away from the edge!', and generally driving everyone insane – as well as heightening the likelihood of someone falling into the water.

Now, however, I have learned to take a step back. I recognise my limitations, and I steer clear of these excursions. I completely trust Ray to mind the children, knowing that they are in safe hands. I love the fact that they are having the time of their lives, and instead I will go for a long walk, making sure to get back in enough time for there to be plenty of hot water and a meal almost ready for their return. I also apply this policy to water parks, climbs up Carrantuohill mountain and all those other risky adventures that boys love.

What I like about the pieces in this chapter is the way each one reveals the very different characters of the individuals involved, while highlighting at the same time the importance they all place on approaching life with a sense of humour. Vincent Browne speaks of the prospect of heaven with a certain wry humour, while extolling the virtues of porter and boiled potatoes and the here-and-now. David Norris describes himself as '*quite naughty*', since, even when he's championing causes, he '*always makes sure to walk on one pair of corns while campaigning*'. Ronan Conroy relies on a mischievous sense of fun and Patsy McGarry on the power of stoic humour and defiant optimism to triumph in even the grimmest of circumstances and regardless of the odds.

In these and all of the other contributions that follow, there is a very real awareness of the importance of living for the joy of living.

The world is full of joy and wonder all around us. We just have to open our eyes and see.

VINCENT BROWNE

I HAVE BEEN ASKED TO WRITE about my philosophy for living, my motivations and the source of my happiness.

A philosophy for living? What's that? I live because I am alive and I think I enjoy living better than I would enjoy being dead. I do not believe in heaven or hell. Anyway, if there is a hell, from what one hears about it, it seems uninviting, although probably most of the people I most enjoy will end up there. If there is a heaven, from what one hears about it, I think I would be bored out of my mind after a weekend there. Hate harp music. As for the people who are probably there, and are likely to get there, aside from Fr Peter McVerry and Sr Stan, I would prefer to be at a Fine Gael Ard Fheis. Missing out on the presence of God, no problem. From what I hear of him, I don't think we would get along.

Pity they privatised purgatory.

Motivation? Motivation for living? See the above.

Source of happiness? Living, family, friends, Limerick (aka Munster) rugby, Broadford/Drumcollogher winning the

All–Ireland Football Club Championship, pints of porter, red wine, boiled potatoes and not bothering my head about a philosophy for living.

Vincent Browne is from Broadford, County Limerick. He is a broadcaster and journalist.

David Norris

ONE OF MY GREAT PALS IS James Joyce's only surviving nephew, Ken Monaghan. We share a nostalgic taste for swing bands, jazz and music of the 1940s. I remember a little while ago, when I was still recovering from a serious illness, Ken sat beside me in the Cobalt Café, with the two of us singing, '*You've got to accentuate the positive, eliminate the negative ...*' That, I think; is a fairly good rough guide to getting on.

Certainly I have always believed that it is important to accentuate the positive and live for the joy of living in this still magnificent world, despite all man's depredations. Of course, one cannot always entirely or instantly eliminate the negative, nor would it be wise to attempt to do so. You have to confront the negative and the difficulties in life squarely, fully and honestly. That is the way to eliminate them. The biggest danger is ignoring them. That's what was wrong with that silly old pill, Lord Denning, when he refused to face what he called the '*appalling vista*' of police corruption, thereby neatly leaving it in place and turning his face against the righting of an injustice.

Righting injustices can be very stimulating, because you are both accentuating the positive and eliminating the negative. By putting energy into good causes, you get a tremendous feeling of self-fulfilment and satisfaction. I don't mean just by being a goody-goody, God knows I'm not. In fact, I am often quite naughty when I am championing causes and I always make sure to walk on at least one pair of corns when campaigning. I find the squeals of my opponents really stimulating!

But you do really get back what you put in. As the Bible says: '*Cast your bread upon the waters, and it will return to you a hundredfold*', and that, of course, is what the Christina Noble Children's Foundation does and continues to do to this day. That is why so many people from radically different backgrounds and perspectives conspire together to support it.

David Norris is a human rights campaigner and a proud Dubliner. He was born in central Africa, but for thirty years has been a resident of the north inner city, where he has been restoring an eighteenth-century house.

GARRET FITZGERALD

HAPPINESS AND PLEASURE ARE TWO QUITE distinct phenomena. Pleasure is essentially an introvert phenomenon, whereas happiness derives from the external factor of our relationships with others.

Our relationships with our families and friends are, for many people - and especially for those lucky enough to have a warm relationship with their partner and their children and friends - a major, I would say primary, source of happiness. And, despite the fact that in an important minority of cases, breakdowns occur in such relationships, most people enjoy this kind of happiness.

Beyond that, many people also find happiness in contributing to the welfare of others - if they are lucky, in a career of service, for example, medicine, teaching or even politics! And for those whose careers don't fall into these categories, there is always the possiblility of spending some of their leisure time engaging in activities of benefit to others.

None of this precludes also having fun. Life should never be allowed to become entirely serious! For my own part, I find the company of people with a sense of the ridiculous and a certain capacity for frivolity and humour to be an important additional source of happiness, especially if they also have a capacity for warmth in their personal relationships.

Garret FitzGerald spent twelve years as an official at Aer Lingus, and subsequently worked as a consultant and university lecturer. Later he entered political life, appearing in the Senate and in the Dáil as Minister for Foreign Affairs in 1973. He became Leader of Fine Gael in 1977 and Taoiseach in 1981. After a brief interval in opposition in 1982, he served as Taoiseach for four years from 1982-87.

RONAN CONROY

The Silent Spitfires

I HEARD A FEATURE ON THE radio about a group who go about trying to 'capture' ghosts on audio tape. They leave a tape recorder running all night in a place that might be haunted, and then listen to the tape for signs. Sometimes, they said, you can hear soft whispering or sighing.

The group had made a recording in a museum, inside an old Second World War bomber. They played a section of the tape. There were clicking sounds which, they said, could have been the sounds of a pilot testing the cockpit switches before taking off. I thought it sounded like an old aircraft creaking a little as the temperature fell.

We found one of these Second World War museums quite by chance, driving through Kent, taking what looked like a shortcut along roads so narrow that we wondered what would happen if we met a car coming in the opposite direction. We didn't meet any traffic at all, in fact. And then we found ourselves in a tiny village – no more than a couple of houses and a pub. Not a soul visible. In the bright morning sunshine, the place was utterly silent.

The aerodrome was right next to the village. Nissen huts, old military vehicles parked outside – exactly like in those endless sunny days of the Battle of Britain. The runway was gone. It started then ended abruptly in a cornfield. But all the buildings were there. We paid our entrance fee to a man in a dapper blazer, and started walking around. We were the only visitors. We fell silent too.

There were clothes shop dummies, looking as if they had been salvaged from long-closed drapers' shops – dressed as pilots, women's airforce ratings, land girls, military police. They were so young, all of them, I thought. Teenagers mostly, fighting a desperate war.

And, of course, the aircraft: the dogged Hurricane, the elegant Spitfire, as well as a patiently restored Messerschmitt 109 that had been shot down by one of the pilots from the squadron. How small and fragile the planes looked. Rolls Royce Merlin and Daimler-Benz engines silent now.

We drifted back together eventually and found ourselves chatting to the man in the blazer. He had been a pilot in the War (I am also one of these people who says 'the War'), flying Spitfires from this very airbase. When he heard we were Irish, he smiled. They had had an Irish pilot in the squadron, he told us. Fine pilot, he recalled, 'Kept us all in suits.' Cloth was scarce, he explained. So when the Irish pilot went home on leave (had to travel in mufti, of course: some of the Irish wouldn't have thought too highly of an RAF uniform), he would return with suit lengths of cloth. Each pilot got a turn to order fabric from Ireland.

'So many remarkable people here in those days,' our guide said wistfully, 'I often wonder what happened to them. We all just seemed to lose touch when the war was over, don't know why.' And he fell silent.

We left. Behind us, the aerodrome sat quietly in the sunshine. No other visitors had arrived, and I wondered what the guide was doing, surrounded by the sights of the war and the silence of the cornfields.

I have often thought about those tape recordings, and how they are missing the point. The ghostly swishes they hear on the tape have simple and obvious explanations. It is the silence, the empty silence inside those cockpits that is the terrible thing. It is there that the ghosts live.

Married to One of the Moors Murderers

I taught in Milltown Institute of Theology and Philosophy. I was in the Philosophy faculty. Between philosophers and theologians, there was no telling what sort of coffee break conversation you would have.

One Friday, the staff room was unusually merry. One of the other lecturers told me the story. It seemed that the previous night, there had been a meeting of prominent members of the Catholic laity, and that some of the theologians had been invited. Over refreshments afterwards, one wealthy and success-ful businessman was complaining loudly. 'Why can't ordinary people see,' he asked, 'that whatever happens is God's will, and is all for the best?'

'I don't know,' said the theologian. 'I reckon that believing in God is more like being married to one of the Moors mur-derers. When He comes home in the evening, you give Him His tea. But you don't ever ask Him what He did today.'

Ernie Gébler at the End

Ernie Gébler's books are long out-of-print. I have never read one. Ernie is remembered now, if at all, as the subject of a rather bitter memoir by his son, who is also a writer.

Ernie was friends with the family of my childhood sweet-heart, and I remember him slightly, at parties in their house: a funny, likeable man who sang melodiously at a time when people still sang at parties.

Val, my childhood sweetheart's mother, told me this story about Ernie's last days. Ernie suffered from dementia and, at the end of his life didn't really recognise people. It pained Val to visit him and see this man, whose sharpness of mind had been legendary, now mostly unable to make out what was going on around him.

It got to the stage when he was really unable to respond, and seemed only semi-conscious. 'But,' said Val, 'I would talk to him anyway, because you don't know, do you, how much a person still understands at some level?'

'One day,' she continued, 'I was talking to him and I mentioned that I had just finished reading a book by his son. I told him that his son was a very good writer indeed. And Ernie suddenly sat up in bed and looked at me – straight at me – and said: "Is he – do you really think so?" I got quite a shock, but I said: "Yes, I really thought he was very good." "Good," said Ernie, "Good."

The moment of lucidity passed almost as quickly as it had come,' Val concluded, 'and Ernie sank back into the bed. He never spoke to me again before he died.'

The Glicks in Life and in Death

There was a chemist's shop for many years in Rathgar called Glick's. It was run by Mr Glick, who had arrived in Ireland from somewhere in middle Europe many years ago. 'Glick' in Gaelic means cunning, or clever in a self-interested way. Customers would find themselves taken aback when Mr Glick would say to them, 'And do you know what my name means in Gaelic?' They would pretend not to know. 'It means upright, or honest,' he would tell them proudly. 'A customer of mine told me so.' And all his life, not one person told him the truth.

Mr and Mrs Glick grew older, together with their little dog, whom they loved. And their one concern, which they often confided in people, was that one of them would die before the others. Neither of the Glicks could imagine life without the other, or without their little dog.

And so it was that one chilly winter's night, the Glicks, man, wife and dog, retired to bed where, in the course of the night, their electric blanket caught fire, silently filling the room with white smoke, which smothered all three while they slept.

About These Things

I had the good fortune, as a teenager, to spend a lot of time in the house of my sweetheart, Maev Kennedy. There, around the kitchen table, everyone told stories, and everyone, young or old, was expected to have a story to tell. It gave me a fondness for listening to people's stories, and retelling them. Looking at them, these stories don't have any educational value at all. They are just stories about people. It's what we're fond of, we Irish.

Professor Ronan Conroy is an ageing, grey-haired figure with a comical moustache, on a bicycle, tracing a regular route between school, crèche and his place of work, the Statistics Department of the Royal College of Surgeons in Ireland. He is the one on the bicycle, of course, not the moustache. That would be silly!

PATSY McGARRY

I WOULD HAVE TO PICK A particular song to illustrate those essential ingredients – humour and defiant optimism – that can be so effective in 'getting through', whether life in general or its occasional acute crises. The song is also outrageously irreverent, which helps!

I refer of course to 'Always Look on the Bright Side of Life' from Monty Python's 1979 film, *The Life of Brian*, now frequently referred to as the greatest British comedy film of all time. You hardly need me to rehash the scene, but we have Brian Cohen, a young Jew mistaken for the Messiah, hanging crucified with an estimated 140 others like him, when a fellow sufferer on a nearby cross begins to sing, 'Always Look on the Bright Side of Life'. It is so ludicrous in the circumstances that the immediate response is usually an explosive laugh – and there is no better medicine.

The song is frequently sung at football matches these days, usually to taunt the other side. But did you know that, in 1982, during the Falklands War, sailors on the British destroyer HMS *Sheffield*, which had been very badly damaged by an Argentinian Exocet missile, sang it while waiting to be rescued? These men recognised that, beneath the humour of the song's apparently frivolous verses, there is a strong note of defiance in the face of seeming overwhelming adversity. It embodies nothing less than a primitive, determined will to survive – half the battle, in any context.

For life is quite absurd
And death's the final word
You must always face the curtain with a bow
Forget about your sin –
Give the audience a grin
Enjoy it – it's your last chance anyhow.

So, always look on the bright side of death
Just before you draw your terminal breath

Life's a piece of shit
When you look at it
Life's a laugh and death's a joke – it's true.
You'll see it's all a show
Keep 'em laughing as you go
Just remember that the last laugh is on you.

And, always look on the bright side of life.
Always look on the right side of life ...

from 'Always Look on the Bright Side of Life'
by Eric Idle, 1979

Sanitised versions of the song, particularly in the US, have altered the line '*Life's a piece of shit*' to '*Life's a counterfeit*', or '*Life is hit or miss*', so as to lessen the likelihood of it offending more rarified sensibilities. But you have to wonder whether sheltering sensibilities from the cruder aspects of this life will be of any benefit to them. Or anyone. Meanwhile, '*Always look on the bright side of life, dee dah, dee dah, dee dah dee dah ...*'

Patsy McGarry is Religious Affairs Correspondent for The Irish Times. *From Ballaghadreen, Co. Roscommon, and a graduate of the National University of Ireland Galway, Patsy holds dear to the impossible dream of his native county winning an All-Ireland Senior Football Championship – just once! – in his lifetime. It last did so in 1944, before he was born.*

Rita Ann Higgins

THE WAITING AREA IN MALAGA AIRPORT is limited, so if you have two hours to kill, a quiet corner to yourself is a bit ambitious. I have a good book and a cup of tea, so on a pleasure scale I'm doing pretty well already. It is noisy, though, and there does not seem to be any place for the noise to go. It hangs in the air over your head, it's very loud and raucous and when the sounds beat off each other, they take on a surreal quality, more like squawking birds doing battle than people chatting.

At intervals, people start pouring out of Arrivals and falling into the arms of their loved ones. I had no idea that watching people greeting each other could be such a moving experience. I watch every loving collision as it happens.

I find myself thinking about the curious intimacy of the hug, its safe and reassuring effect. Some huggers are so passionate, it makes me tearful. It's so real, and spontaneous. Some huggers make your breathing change to an uneven beat. I start to think about good huggers. Do I know any good huggers? Can I remember the best hug I've have ever had? Some huggers hoop as well as hug. Some huggers clap the recipient on the back as well as hug. So many emotions are running side by side: they are reflected on the faces of those waiting for the loved ones to walk through that door. The emotions vary from fear and anxiety to pure joy.

I'm thinking about a hug I once had that lasted what seemed like an eternity but it probably wasn't for very long. It was tender and secure with a clear message of friendship, it was never topped.

Some get hugged and some are huggers. Some might be great huggers but not while they have an audience. Some huggers need an audience. Often people break ranks and run under the fence, so to speak, usually grandmothers on seeing their loving grandchildren.

At Malaga airport, you are allowed to bring your dog in and there is nothing like the excitement a dog displays when it sees its owner walking through those doors.

Dogs aside, the lovers' hug is an entirely different matter. They hug and kiss and stand back and 'let me look at you', and more hugs and more kisses. You can tell the lovers a mile off. When teenagers meet here, they 'flock-hug' and almost spin each other into San Pedro: they are loud, but this time it's a nice loud, an approved-of loud.

The reason why someone waits at Arrivals at an airport is pretty obvious, but the strange mechanisms and energy that float around as you hug or immediately after you are embraced are not so easy to define. The most striking and powerful action, when people are hugging, is that arms are outstretched to draw a loved one closer for a flash-lightning second or seconds, seconds that can never ever be measured in real time. The hug is an action that may not warrant another thought, a phenomenon that brings about closeness, something intangible which enhances our ability to give and receive affection.

Thoughts haven't time to finish themselves, chaos and giddiness set in, the Arrival doors are opened, and they're off. Some time ago, I came across this quotation, but I don't know who wrote it: *'It takes four hugs a day to survive, eight hugs a day to maintain and twelve hugs a day to grow.'*

Malaga, Oh Malaga

Rita Ann Higgins, 2009

I am a goose on one leg
waiting at Malaga airport
no one will notice that I'm a goose
because Malaga airport is full of geese
standing on one leg
and it's always the left leg.

The noise at Malaga airport has a cadence
a loud loud lisp
and a cac cac cackle,
all thunder, no rain.

Some noises are necessary
if we want to see the other birds,
and we all want to see the other birds,
we have to put up with the noise.
Aren't we making half the noise ourselves,
so many geese together,
so many wild geese.

I stick my neck out.
I have a neck like a swan,
a shrink once told me.
My father used to say
I had a neck for anything but soap.
I stick my neck out to see
if the other bird has landed,
the rest do the same thing,
they stick their necks out.

The odd cratur hops on the other foot,
but we take no notice,
hardly anyone hisses
except two old codgers
who fell fowl of the flock years ago.
They were leaning against the back wall,
complaining about air miles
and the journey south,
scratching their tail feathers.

You could forgive them that,
this waiting is wearing on the nerves,

loved ones are coming for Christmas,
the expectations terrify,
the noise is now more whooper
than hubbub.
It blocks out everything,
except what the eyes can see,
all the eyes are on the Arrivals gate
and on the electronic notice board
landed, delayed, landed, delayed,
landed delayed landed
which is it, which is it,
we all stretch our swans necks.

It's hardly a sanctuary here,
but all those open arms
harness their own remedy
a veinless, threadless remedy
that needs no water or air to flourish,
just those outstretched arms
and a dash of something,
unseen unheard
made from lonely,
made from loss.

We were alone for nine hundred years,
now all those loving collisions
are turning us into right ninnies,
we are sobbing and bobbing
and all-over happy and sad and secure,
but our clothes are all creased,

and the teenagers aren't cygnets anymore
but they are still whooping,
and the noise is all thunder, no rain,
people are getting hugged
right, left and centre, arms outstretched
loving collisions are happening,
feathers are flying
all over Malaga airport.

Rita Ann Higgins was born in Galway in 1955, and divides her time between Galway and Spiddal. She has written numerous collections of poetry and plays. She was Galway County's Writer-in-Residence in 1987, Writer-in-Residence in NUI Galway 1994-95, and Writer-in-Residence for Offaly County Council 1998-99. Rita Ann was Green Honors Professor at Texas Christian University in October 2000 and was made an Honorary Fellow at Hong Kong Baptist University in 2006.

KINDNESS

KINDNESS IS AN ESSENTIAL INGREDIENT for happiness. The essence of leading a happy life is surely to try to weave threads of kindness through our daily existence. I find that it is those small acts of generosity and love bestowed on me, and which I can bestow on others that make each day worthwhile.

Francis Brennan mentions in his contribution that one of the things he would most like as his legacy would be for it to be said that he '*made people happy*'. I think that is a wonderful maxim for managing our daily lives: finding opportunities to make others happy.

The piece by Professor Tony Scott is very special to me, because of the great kindness he has shown me in the past. I can still remember walking into Tony's office as a seventeen-year-old one summer afternoon, explaining to him that I wanted to do a project on spiders for the Young Scientist of the Year competition. My idea was to investigate the strength and elasticity of the fibres in spiders' webs. Tony spent the entire afternoon on the phone with various experts in physics, before we came up with a template and several formulae that would enable me to test my ideas.

When the news came that I had won the competition, the first person to congratulate me, when all the fuss had died down, was Tony. I can still remember his face, wreathed in smiles, as he gave me a big hug at the presentation ceremony in the RDS, all those years ago. He couldn't have been more delighted than if he had won that prize himself!

Michael Meegan's contribution is one of my favourites in this section. Each line is a gem, as Michael highlights the need '*to restore ourselves in silence*', the sense in which we can choose our experiences and, most importantly of all, as he reveals '*the secret*': '*The less we think of ourselves and distract ourselves, the more we have time to listen and delight in the gift of each other.*'

> *Allow the Lord, by love and grace,*
> *to let you live this moment,*
> *right now.*
> *This moment is as perfect as it*
> *can be.*
> *And God's call, the needs of the*
> *world, will make themselves*
> *very apparent.*
> *Just respond to the need that*
> *presents itself right in front of*
> *you today.*

Anon.

MICHAEL MEEGAN

LIFE IS A CONSTANT SURPRISE, THROWING at us all sorts of challenges and dramas. News floods us with all the bad things happening: wars, meltdown, rising costs, political fights. It's easy to become discouraged. We navigate through our own day, coping with the pressures and stresses of an uncertain future. Sometimes, all of this can bring pain into our lives, all sorts of pain. Worry, fear, doubt, sadness – these are types of pain. Loss, rejection and confusion create feelings within us that need to be dulled.

We are in an addicted society, addicted to numbing ourselves. There are socially allowable addictions: cynicism, sarcasm, the pub, work, being busy, eating, keeping that 'forward' motion, but, like more obvious addictions, these painkillers also damage us. Anything that keeps us from understanding the nature of our inner pain prevents us from removing it. Like physical pain, we experience suffering in all its forms for a reason. Instead of distracting ourselves with noise, we need to rekindle the art of listening, of becoming still. We have become strangers to ourselves.

At the heart of many cultures and disciplines lies this simple insight: that we restore ourselves in silence. The problem, of course, is that, for most of us, silence is anything but still. If we turn off the noise, stop being busy, stop being caught up, what we experience can be a tidal wave of thoughts. This flood of 'being in our own heads' can be uncomfortable. We are so used to 'fast-forward' that when we stop, we become agitated. We can make a choice. We can choose to give ourselves a gift, a gift of something we never seem to have: a little time. Give yourself ten minutes a day, without distractions – no phone, no work, no music or background static. Turn off the stuff, all of it. As you try that, you will find that you grow more and more comfortable with that inner space. In time, this will change not only how you are within yourself, but how you are with yourself.

Experience is choice. We can choose to shop less, we can choose our words, choose to listen more, we can decide to become more patient. In the tiny threads that make up the fabric of this day, there is a choice behind every action and every word, and a freedom behind every action and every thought.

This letting go is, in many ways, a freeing of ourselves from the cycles and traps that create pain. It is discovering the gift of the present moment, the only thing we can control in our lives. This can start with the smallest expression, it grows in every word we choose to use, it is in every act of goodness. It is true that it can be a frightening world out there: it can be lonely and we can often feel vulnerable. We are easily hurt, and every one of us needs more tenderness, more understanding and more kindness. As we let go of the distractions, the 'stuff', we make more space in our lives to celebrate, to rejoice, to create the little acts of caring that bring hope and light to each other.

Nothing heals the soul more deeply than kindness. The secret is that the less we think of ourselves and distract ourselves, the more we have time to listen and delight in the gift of each other. At the heart of joy and healing lies forgiveness, and the first person we need to forgive is often ourselves. As we face the many challenges unfolding in our world, it is of lasting value to remember such simple things.

There are many ways of numbing pain, but stillness will help to awaken a deeper part of us. Real change is in the little things we do here and now, in the smallest choices. The more we choose to be awake, the more we will celebrate and see grace and wonder. Forgiveness is the gate, compassion is the path, and love the reason for being alive.

Michael Meegan is International Director of the International Community for Relief of Starvation and Suffering, and the author of several inspirational books, including All will be Well. *Michael has spent almost thirty years living among the Masai in Kenya.*

CATHY KELLY

CHILDREN INSTINCTIVELY KNOW HOW TO BE happy. They make it look so simple. They find pleasure in the simplest things, be it a sticky bun with a cup of milk, or curling up on the couch with people they love, hugging and laughing. They are themselves, and don't try to be something they're not. What you see is what you get.

If children like something, they say so. If they don't like something, they say that too. They laugh until they have a pain in their stomachs, they smile and turn their faces up to the sun when it comes out, and they admire the stars at night, finding wonder in the night sky. If they are sad, they cry until the sadness is gone. Every feeling and thought is trusted. When children are loved and happy, they are emotionally healthy little beings, because, knowing themselves to be loved, they love themselves too. 'I matter,' they think. 'I am important to the people in my life.'

It's taken me many years to figure it out, but living with a child-like appreciation of life and yourself is one of the simplest ways to be happy. Of course, this doesn't always work, and many people have lives with great pain within, where a simple philosophy isn't quite enough. But when it is applicable, it is fantastic.

We grown-ups don't always say what we think: we hide our anxieties and worry that our fears will appear foolish. We don't say what we mean for a variety of complicated reasons. We are often scared that what we feel and think don't matter. We try to behave in certain ways because we are afraid that who we truly are isn't loveable or is, in some indefinable way, wrong. And yet this isn't a blueprint for happy living, while the childlike way is.

After over forty years on the planet, I now see that all the best moments of my life have come about from living in a way that children recognise. Like being my true self, trusting this wonderful universe around me, sending kindnesses back out there. As long as it isn't going to hurt someone, I try to say what I think. I do my best to say what comes from within. That's how I write too: by being as authentic as I can. It's not necessarily right or wrong, it's simply what I think. It's what children do instinctively, and they're right.

I do my best to help other people, because the joy I get from that makes me so very happy. Like a child putting money in a charity box to help other children in poverty around the world, I try to think of the world in 'micro terms'. Children believe they're helping the smiling child on the charity poster. That makes them put their copper coins in the collection box. The same method works for me too.

If today I can make a difference in one person's life – like a child in Africa through UNICEF, or a child in Belarus through Chernobyl Children's Project International – then I feel so proud for helping another human being.

Being kind to one person is a child's pure viewpoint of the world. Feeling negative about all the wrongs of the world, and therefore feeling that you can help nobody, will not benefit anyone.

My philosophies are kindness, honesty and being able to laugh at myself when I'm wrong, which happens all the time. I'm always making mistakes. I just try to make different ones rather than the same ones again!

There will always be days when it all goes wrong, when good thoughts appear to mean nothing and bad things happen. That's life. How we deal with it is what makes us different from all the other creatures on the planet.

But, in the meantime, I'm trying to smile and be in touch with the little person inside me who loves the sunshine, watches the moon with awe and loves a good belly laugh.

Cathy Kelly is a number one international bestselling author. She worked as a journalist before becoming a novelist, and has published eleven novels, including her current title Once in a Lifetime. *Cathy is an ambassador for UNICEF Ireland, and a patron of Chernobyl Children's Project International. She lives in Wicklow with her partner and their twin sons.*

Seamus Heaney

'St Kevin and the Blackbird' is a poem which embodies something like my own philosophy of life. The story is a beautiful little fable about doing unto others as you would have them do unto you.

St Kevin and the Blackbird

from *The Spirit Level* by
Seamus Heaney, 1996

And there was St Kevin and the blackbird.
The saint was kneeling, arms stretched
out, inside
His cell, but the cell is narrow, so

One turned-up palm is out the
window, stiff
As a crossbeam, when a blackbird lands
And lays in it and settles down to nest.

Kevin feels the warm eggs, the small
breast, the tucked

Neat head and claws and, finding
himself linked
Into the network of eternal life,

Is moved to pity: now he must
hold his hand
Like a branch out in the sun and rain
for weeks
Until the young are hatched and fledged
and flown.

And since the whole thing's
imagined anyhow,
Imagine being Kevin. Which is he?
Self-forgetful, or in agony all the time

From the neck on out down through
his hurting forearms?
Are his fingers sleeping? Does he feel his
knees?
Or has the shut-eyed blank of
underearth

Crept up through him? Is there distance
in his head?
Alone and mirrored clear in love's
deep river.
'To labour and not to seek reward,'
he prays,

A prayer his body makes entirely
For he has forgotten self, forgotten bird
And on the riverbank forgotten the
river's name.

Seamus Heaney was born in Co. Derry in Northern Ireland. Death of a Naturalist, his first collection of poems, appeared in 1966, and since then he has published poetry, criticism and translations, including Beowulf and District and Circle. He was awarded the Nobel Prize in Literature in 1995. Stepping Stones, a book of interviews with Denis O'Driscoll, was published in 2008.

Patricia Casey

As the poet Robert Burns wrote: '*Man's inhumanity to man makes countless thousands mourn.*' And man's inhumanity is visible everywhere, from Guantánamo Bay to the killing of the powerless and defenceless. On our own doorstep in times of plenty, or perhaps because of it, we experience it with dismal and depressing frequency. We see the internecine fighting between factions and gangs that has led to the maiming of children and the wanton destruction of innocent bystanders.

Less graphic than bloodshed, but troubling to those who believe in the absolute value of every person, we see the worth of people being measured by their intellectual prowess, by wealth or physical attractiveness or by values that are ephemeral and utilitarian.

Against this vista, it is easy to be duped into believing that evil is making inexorable progress and that unconditional regard for humanity is being eroded, eventually drowning out the cries of those who beg for shelter, for food, for compassion and for healing. But there are many, usually silent and perhaps easily forgotten, who ought to be remembered for what another great poet, William Wordsworth, referred to as their '*little, unremembered acts of kindness*' towards those who are vulnerable and needy.

There are the people who do soup runs to the homeless on our streets, who stand up for the downtrodden and fight injustice. The ones who by their actions proclaim the infinite value of humanity. It is they who unknowingly challenge the smugness and callousness that is around us, who erode the progress of wickedness and who are towering monuments to the inherent goodness of people.

Patricia Casey is Professor of Psychiatry at UCD and Consultant Psychiatrist at the Mater Hospital, Dublin. She is the author of five books and has contributed to over forty. She also writes a weekly column, 'Mind and Meaning', for the Irish Independent, *and is a regular contributor to the media in general. Patricia's research has led her to involvement in studies on suicide, deliberate self-harm and stress reactions.*

Tony Scott

Some people believe in fate, good fortune or simply luck. I am of the opinion that such things are of one's own making. I was certainly fortunate that I went to a school where the teachers made subjects not just educational, but interesting as well. So, for me, a career as an academic scientist was almost a natural consequence, having been inspired as I had been by my teachers to study physics.

The twin aspects for an academic of teaching and research were both sources of fulfilment and great enjoyment. Research had its own excitement, in the opportunity to follow a path where perhaps no one had been before. Teaching was pure satisfaction: coming out from a lecture to perhaps 300 students, at which you sensed and even believed you had succeeded in getting a somewhat complex concept understood, was a reward in itself.

Having been involved with the Young Scientist Exhibition for over 40 years, I have always found meeting and talking with enthusiastic young people a pleasure. Their desire to tell you about their discoveries while working on their project always made me look forward to the dull and cold days of January.

My father tried to instil in me a need to help others, but with this addendum, 'When you do some kind act for an individual or group, do not wait around to be lauded, but rather drift quietly into the background.' It is a guiding principle I always try to follow. The inner satisfaction of having achieved something, be it helping someone, or finishing a successful piece of research or a lecture that students benefited from, is reward in itself.

I live a contented life, being grateful for what I have, happy in the career that I follow, and surrounded by good memories and good friends. Whether this is due to fate, good fortune or luck, I will leave others to judge.

A Dubliner, Tony Scott received his early education in Terenure College. He then graduated from UCD with a degree in Experimental Physics. Subsequently commencing research in Atmospheric Physics, he was awarded an MSc and, later, a PhD. Appointed to the staff of the Physics Department at UCD, Tony later served as Dean of the Faculty of Science. Always interested in promoting science to young people, he has been involved in the Young Scientist Exhibition since its inception in 1965.

Breda O'Brien

ALL OF US HAVE IDEALS TO which we aspire, and I know I often fail miserably to come anywhere near my own. As I get older and some of my children are beginning the accelerating gallop to adulthood, I have begun to think that kindness is one of the great underrated virtues. I know that any time I have descended to being patronising or cutting, I have undermined the validity of any argument I was attempting to make. In the media however, there is a culture of cool irony, a relentless mockery of idealism that sometimes degenerates into biting, personalised attacks.

Kindness costs. It can mean appearing weak, or naïve or vulnerable. It most certainly is not cool. However, kindness is like balm to a wounded spirit, and even when it appears to be spurned, I believe that it is never wasted. When my shy, quiet mother died, it was only at her funeral that I learned of her numerous gentle acts of kindness, never forgotten by neighbours.

Kindness is not easy, and for some of us, we fail more often than we succeed. Perhaps that is why I find forgiveness so closely allied to kindness. And while I referred to common courtesy, if there is one concept our age finds quainter than kindness, it is surely courtesy. And yet we have never been more in need of kindness, or indeed courtesy, to render our daily lives together not just bearable, but both human and fulfilling.

Breda O'Brien is a teacher at Muckross Park College and a colum-
nist with The Irish Times.

FRANCIS BRENNAN

I AM NOT HAPPY. IT IS 31 December, the busiest night of the year in the hotel world, and I have just caused angst where there should be joy.

Do you ever notice that there are 'happy' people peppered throughout the world whom, I have no doubt, are put here for the purpose of lifting spirits as they go about their daily lives? They could be the tea lady in the office, the rural postman on his daily rounds, or indeed a DJ on the radio.

I like to think that I have been blessed with a touch of this magic – but tonight, not so. My young nephew, of eleven years, was 'allowed' to attend the New Year's Eve Gala Ball for the first time, and join his cousins visiting from Sligo. This was a surprise for him, as he had no notion or desire to attend. His cousin, aged ten, appeared at my office, resplendent in the smallest tuxedo ever made, I'd say. Shortly thereafter, my nephew arrived in civvies, albeit a Tommy Hilfiger sweater and polo shirt, and I, believing that he must be intending to change clothes, ask him if he would like a room for same. The minute I said it, I knew by the look on his face that I had shattered his joy at having been invited to the ball. It is one of my failings at times to be too quick to comment, be it good or bad.

Over the years, I have been blessed by having many of those 'happy' people work with me here at the hotel. These people come to work perpetually happy and, by being so, lift all with them on the tide of a funny incident from the evening before, or something on the television or indeed the observance of something on the way to work. They radiate a happiness that permeates all. They say the Lord works in strange ways, and I honestly believe that He has a particular hand in the creation of those who radiate such joy and happiness. Whether it has been stimulated by some event in their lives when they were young, or parents that instilled an air of happiness in them, or their first teacher, these so blessed are 'daily specials' in all our lives.

Tonight, I did not live up to my usual role. But when people ask me, as they often do, what I would like my legacy to be, I always reply, that I was a good employer, I made people happy and that I was blessed with a great faith. Tonight, I learned that it is not easy to be 'kind' all the time, that one has to strive harder daily.

And, by the way, as I left the hotel at 1.55 a.m., with a receding pain in my stomach, I noticed my eleven-year-old nephew dancing away with a big smile on his face. Youth has a great ability to bounce back – thank the Lord! However, unbeknownst to themselves, they can also teach us that a kind word, rather than a harsh one, goes a long way towards a happier world. So I have learned tonight.

Francis Brennan is the Proprietor of the Park Hotel, Kenmare, and a winner of the Egon Ronay Hotel of the Year. In 2004, he developed the Samas Destination Spa, regarded as the forerunner for spa development in Europe, and which has been acclaimed as one of the top ten of its kind in Europe, and has won other many accolades besides. He is currently developing the Retreats, a modern living complex adjacent to the Park Hotel, which features interiors by London designer, David Linley.

KATHY SINNOTT

Extra Layers

THERE WAS A MOMENT. IT WAS when the icy bed had finally warmed directly around me that I felt safe. I would like to have spent more time in this moment but, with its arrival, I fell asleep.

In the morning, I was still in the capsule of warmth, but it was no longer safe, just hard to leave. My first waking thoughts were already focused on the problems of the new day.

It was not so much the lack of money, because thirty years ago a family could survive on very little. There weren't an endless stream of fees, contributions, penalties and charges on everything. Dressing the children and myself was not an issue. Clothes did not have brand names or logos: they came and went from house to house in black bags. Nappies were washable; single tub ringer washing machines were given free by those who had advanced to twin tub. And who ironed?

Gathering scrap wood was a necessity in cold weather, but it became fun too, as a treasure hunt. The search for the best single piece of fire wood went on for several years, with reigning champions ever watchful to maintain their title.

With the help of the wood, a bag of slack and a bag of coal could be made to last from one children's allowance day to the next. A small fire when the children arrived in from school was cheering and kept one room bearable. We didn't worry about the evenings, as we spent those wrapped in blankets in the bed with library books, reading aloud chapters and chapters of adventure. The colder the day, the earlier we headed upstairs to read, and the more stories we got through.

I was not conscious of feeling personally beset. I was very focused on giving my children a childhood. I couldn't keep them from the poverty of our life, but I was determined that it should not be experienced as harsh. More than anything, I wanted my children to have happy memories. They could not go to the cinema or circus, but when the little flat was closing in on us, we could go 'adventuring' – setting off in the Morris Minor, with no plan or destination. We spent the day walking and climbing – but only on the driest days, as the windshield wipers on the car did not work.

I became very good at finding the most nourishment for the smallest price. Liver and heart, cabbage and carrots, and, of course, spuds ... I still love potatoes. I knew what time and which days shops sold off or gave away their ripe fruit. I was such a good customer that some shops kept their pickings just for us. My children thought that only brown speckled bananas were edible. One day, passing a shop, one of my sons wrinkled his nose in distaste, pointing to a window display of perfect green-tinged yellow bananas and saying: 'Mommy, who would buy those?.'

One memory that my children are fond of recalling affectionately is the 'Choose-it Dinner'. Although I could make a little stretch a long way, by the time we reached our last pound, the house had been scoured for loose change, pockets had been turned inside out and the cupboards really were bare. I might have worried about the third and the second last pound, but I refused to worry about the last. What's the point? The last pound is something to enjoy. So when we found ourselves there, we set the table for a party and then all took that pound to the shop, where the children chose dinner. The instant choice was always ice-cream because, outside of a birthday, we never had ice-cream, but they would spend ages deciding whether to get the block of raspberry ripple or plain vanilla. Once home, the festivities would begin, with everyone contributing a joke or story to the dinner conversation until we scraped the last of the creamy rectangle with our spoons.

Later, after the children had finally fallen asleep, this was one evening when I would not allow myself to worry. They say God helps those who help themselves, and I suppose it's true, but the miracles only really start when you realise how much you need God's help, and you ask for it. This night, when the last penny was gone, I would entrust my family completely to Him and go to bed as happy as the children, knowing that somehow tomorrow all would be well. It always was.

We moved to a new corporation house in Hollyhill two days before Christmas. We all had the flu and were so sick that we spent Christmas sleeping on mattresses on the kitchen floor. I had just woken up on St Stephen's Day, weak but hungry, and, looking at the sleeping children around me, was wondering, 'Now what?', when there was a knock on the door.

It was Mr and Mrs McCarthy, with two of their teenage sons, dressed in old work clothes. They brought pots of paint from their shed. No one threw anything away in those days. Mr McCarthy and the lads began painting the bare grey walls, filling the house and thrilling the children with their good-natured slagging. Mrs McCarthy brought a baking pan of turkey and ham, potatoes and carrots. For us, starving after the long fast, it was the best Christmas dinner ever. She also brought a measuring tape. By the end of the week, the house was painted and functional, and there were reworked curtains on all the windows.

Being in a new home alone with my children was isolating that winter, but as soon as the weather warmed, all the mothers came out. We sat on the walls chatting, watching the children play and formed close friendships.

Today, my oldest children love teasing their younger brothers and sisters about their MP3 players and laptops. I listen closely and am thankful that their 'When we were young ...' stories are affectionate and not bitter. It could have gone either way. I have learned that, as a parent, we cannot give a child happy memories. We can only provide love, time and attention, and hope that the child gets what he or she needs from these to form them.

Kathy Sinnott was an Independent member of the European Parliament for Munster from 2004–2009. She has been and continues to be especially active in the areas of disability, family and health. She is Chairperson of the Hope Project, which supports people with disabilities and their families. In 2000, she challenged the state to provide a primary education for her son, Jamie, who has multiple disabilities. In 2001, the High Court ruled that Jamie and every person in Ireland had a constitutional right to primary education, and that this right should be based on need, not age. Kathy is mother to nine children and guardian to seven nieces and nephews.

BRIAN FARRELL

The Sad Shepherd

from the *Wild Swans at Coole*
by WB Yeats, 1919

You sing as always of the natural life,
And I that made like music in
my youth
Hearing it now have sighed for that
young man
And certain lost companions of
my own.

I came to be a coroner as a result of my time as a pathologist in hospital laboratories and autopsy rooms. Contrary to public perception, most of the work of a pathologist is carried out for the benefit of living patients in wards and clinics.

Here, the science of histopathology is utilised in making a tissue diagnosis on biopsy or surgically resected specimens.

Histopathology in the autopsy room is referred to as 'anatomical pathology' or 'morbid anatomy'. Similar techniques are applied to establish the cause of death, but with more emphasis on dissection and 'gross' appearances. This formed an important part of my practice at that time.

This work brought me into contact with bereaved relatives endeavouring to come to terms with the awful experience of a sudden, unnatural or violent death in the family. As the coroner's pathologist, it was often necessary for me to meet with family members to further explain or interpret the autopsy findings, at the inquest, or subsequently.

These experiences provided the motivation for my wish to become a coroner and be actively involved in medico-legal death investigation. It has been my career ambition to assist in the professional development of the coronial service to those whose lives have been touched by tragedy. The vindication of the right to life and the right of families, next-of-kin and society in general to a sensitive, comprehensive and professional death inquiry has been my principal objective.

I have to acknowledge, with regret, that these aspirations are not always met, for a variety of reasons, but they remain central to my modus operandi.

I expect no thanks for doing what is, after all, my job in life, but when family members take the trouble to express their gratitude at having been helped in some small way to bear the overwhelming sorrow for the tragic or untimely death of a loved one, I am awed and humbled by their strength and generosity at such a time.

Dr Brian Farrell is the Dublin City Coroner and past President of the Coroners' Society of Ireland. A former consultant histopathologist and barrister-at-law, he is a member of the Coroners' Society of England and Wales and the International Association of Forensic Toxicologists, and, the only full-time coroner in Ireland. He has served on a number of high-level committees on the Review of the Coroners' Service and Bioethics. Dr Farrell is the author of Coroners: Practice and Procedure.

UNDERSTANDING

I N HIS BOOK, ANAM CARA, JOHN O'Donohue talks about visualising the mind as a tower with lots of windows. He remarks that many people view the world every day through one window, looking at the same scene in the same way. He suggests that real growth and understanding occurs when we draw back and see all the possible different windows from which to view the world.

In a sense, each of the pieces in this section is like another window in the tower of which O'Donohue speaks, with each contributor offering their own very individual perspective on where true happiness lies.

I like the straightforward practicality of Michael O'Flynn's recommendation, '*if you engage positively with people, they will engage positively with you in return.*' This sounds so easy, but so often interaction is hampered by pride, past hurts and petty point-scoring.

Maureen Gaffney talks of '*the science and art of happiness*'. The 'science' of happiness is the theory, the 'art' is this theory put into action, day by day. Happiness does not just happen. It is something at which we must work hard in order to make it a reality in our daily lives.

In a similar vein, clinical psychologist Marie Murray approaches the question of contentment in a very scientific way, offering an objective overview of the very many subjective assessments of what makes for a happy life. Yet her summation of happiness concludes with what could be seen as the wonderfully unscientific paradox that '*our own happiness increases when we give happiness away*.'

Once we understand this, happiness becomes a possibility for us all.

Paul Sreenan

How to be Unhappy

In what, of necessity, is a brief contribution, I am going to leave aside the unhappiness which is the result of the awful condition of depression. I am also not speaking of the unhappiness which is the result of acute loss or trauma. Rather, I am speaking of the sort of happiness or unhappiness that is the result of attitudes of mind over which we may have some control.

For most people, it takes little or no effort to be unhappy. On the other hand, if you want to be happy, you have to work at it. Happiness is not like a university degree that, after you have acquired it, you get to keep. No, it takes effort, constant effort. On the other hand, unhappiness is the default condition that arises when you fail to make that effort.

Happiness is also a product of a combination of personal qualities, whereas any one of a large number of things can on their own make you unhappy. Chief amongst these in my own experience is perfectionism. Perfectionists find it very hard to be happy. Their standards are so high that the chances of them being met are slim. This applies to everything in their lives, from the important, such as relationships and their work product, to the trivial, such as the food in a restaurant or the cleanliness in their home.

Anger is not far removed from perfectionism and, again, is a potent cause of unhappiness. How many people have caused themselves and others so much suffering, because they could not or would not control their anger?

Just these two causes of unhappiness serve to highlight two important points. The first, I have mentioned already. You have to work at being happy. The perfectionist has to work at recognising that the glass is half-full – not half-empty. And we all have to make the effort to acquire the tools to manage anger, so that not giving in to anger becomes second nature and that as a result we will, it is to be hoped, never have to face the destruction and remorse that comes from having reacted violently to some perceived insult, perhaps while drunk, to which we would never have reacted while sober.

The second I have also mentioned briefly: that happiness is the result of a number of personal qualities working together. To my mind, there are nine qualities that can be seen in happy people. First, gratitude. Second, to use a term often referred to in the writings of the inspirational Buddhist monk, Thich Nhat Hanh (to whom I and many thousands of others are deeply indebted) mindfulness. Again, these two qualities are interlinked. A mindful person is deeply aware of the magic of his sight, of the beauty of the world around him, of the commitment, friendship and the work of his spouse, children and those with whom he works. Mindfulness leads to gratitude.

Third is light-heartedness. You can't take life too seriously. A joke a day helps to keep the doctor away. Smiling relieves tension, not just for you, but for those around you. Fourth is kindness. Not a word we frequently use. Those who practise kindness on a daily basis not only make others happy but become happy themselves in the process.

The fifth is closely linked to kindness: understanding. This, in my experience, is the most difficult one because it takes real effort and often has to be practised in adversity. However, without understanding, we cannot be truly kind. Neither can we be compassionate, which is the sixth quality I would identify, which, together with kindness, is almost a natural result of understanding.

The seventh is also important. It is self-love. We have to form a positive view of ourselves and be less dependent on others for praise or friendship, and less susceptible to their criticism. We also have to stop beating ourselves up over our past mistakes and concentrate on the present. The late pope John XXIII was fond of an inscription that can be found in the church in the town of his birth, the first section of which referred to: '*three past things – the evil done, the good left undone and the time wasted*'. We also have to let go of past mistakes and traumas if we are to be truly happy.

The next quality again is linked to the others. It is freedom of the mind. Freedom from cravings for possessions, people, food, freedom from addictions, freedom from blaming others for where or what we are. The freedom of realising that you, not others, are responsible for your own happiness. Freedom from jealousy. Freedom from dependence on others – and what they do and say – to make you happy.

Finally, there is peace. A lot of unhappiness is born of fear and anxiety, both rational and irrational. Peace does not just happen. You have to work at it. My own path involves my Christian faith, spirituality, prayer and meditation, but others will follow different paths just as effectively. For many, peace is the result of the other qualities of gratitude, light-heartedness, mindfulness, kindness, understanding, compassion, self-love and freedom.

The thing about happiness and unhappiness is that they are both infectious. Both affect others around us. That means that we owe it to ourselves and others to follow the path of happiness and to make the effort that this requires.

Paul Sreenan is a Senior Council, practising in Dublin. Born in Cork, he was educated at Presentation Brothers College and UCC. He now lives in Dublin with his wife, Siobhan, and their three children.

Maureen Gaffney

Understanding the psychological science of happiness is my job. The art of happiness is trying to put it into operation in my own life. These are the strategies that work for me most consistently ...

First, don't be too fearful of challenge and adversity. When asked what would make us happy, most of us offer the same predictable list – some variety of enjoyment, success or improvement in our life circumstances. Yet, when asked to reflect on what has actually meant most to us in our lives, what has made us feel best about ourselves, we produce quite a different list. Almost always, overcoming great personal challenges features on that list.

Successfully confronting adversity has unexpectedly positive outcomes. We discover strengths we never knew we had; we forge unbreakable bonds with those who helped us through; we feel wiser and more in touch with what really matters in life. In short, we discover that we have flourished under fire. So, while we would never wish for it, adversity and challenge produce the deepest kind of happiness.

Second, relish those moments of pure grace that remind you of the abundance of life. In my own case: the ready affection of my children; hill walking in Roundstone last summer, and dancing around the kitchen at night to the music of The Eagles; tasting the last pot of my perfect cherry and orange marmalade; the clouds clearing over the soaring Spire in Dublin's O'Connell Street as I cycle to work. These are moments of pure grace that I want to hold forever.

Third, no matter how negative your mood, you are simultaneously experiencing positive feelings, although the signals may be weak. Surprisingly, the evidence is that positive and negative states are largely independent systems. The trick is to pay attention to the positive while you are feeling negative. At the very least, there is always a small immediate pleasure to be found using your five senses. I look at our lovely garden, where something is flowering every month of the year, I listen to 'The Benedictus' from *The Armed Man*. I breathe in the smell of an old book, I stroke my sixteen-year-old dog (who is nearly blind and deaf, but still loves her food and a good bark). Or I simply remind myself of those things in my mind's eye – because just thinking about happy memories produces a feeling of happiness almost as intense as the original experience.

Fourth, do something. If I am stuck with a problem and unable to see my way through, I go for a run, or tidy my desk, or e-mail my friends. Sometimes, especially for women, plumbing the depths of a problem is counterproductive. I have come to respect distraction as a way of stealing around unhappiness.

Fifth, remind yourself that, in every situation in life, you have at least some small element of choice. You may not be able to control what happens to you, but you can choose some part of your response. In my own case, I have (nearly successfully) given up comparing myself to other people. Comparing yourself to those better off makes you feel bad, while comparing yourself to those worse off offers only temporary consolation.

Finally, it really is worth learning to be positive – the growing science of happiness may help you here. Not only does it make you feel good, it helps you function better in virtually every domain of life. You will make better decisions and be more creative and more flexible. If you can keep it up, you will build better relationships, have significantly better health and live longer. Seven and a half years longer, actually! That's why I have a page from an old calendar pinned to my wall. It says: '*Don't let yourself get down. Either be up, or getting up.*'

Dr Maureen Gaffney is a well-known psychologist, broadcaster and writer. She is Chair of the National Economic and Social Forum, a board member of the Health Service Executive (HSE), and has served on a number of other boards. She is also a member of the Women's Leadership Board at Harvard University's Kennedy School of Government.

Eileen Dunne

Motivation

I CONSIDER MYSELF A CHILD of the 1970s. I was a teenager and so while Elvis and The Beatles can leave me cold, it's the music of James Taylor and Carole King that has been the soundtrack to my life. Also, 'Desiderata' – an inspirational poem written by an American poet and lawyer, Max Ehrmann, in 1927. It was widely distributed before and during the Second World War, but achieved cult status in the early 1970s, following a recording by television presenter Les Crane, and, along with posters of Che Guevara, it adorned many a bedsit wall in those years.

I left school in 1975, and 'Desiderata' was printed on the back page of our Graduation Mass missalette. What a smart move by the nuns (the Poor Servants of the Mother of God)! Here was something we could identify with, but which also sent us out into the world with some sound advice.

Maybe it's because Ehrmann was a lawyer that his view of the world was so balanced. Some lines stand out, and some mean more to me now than they did back then. However, if I have learned anything over the years, it's that despite all I have learned (and am still learning), goals, principles and traits of character that I set, adhered to and admired in those late teenage years are the ones that matter still!

'Go placidly amid the noise and haste'; *'for always there will be greater and lesser persons than yourself'*; *'be yourself, especially do not feign affection'*: these are lines that come to me frequently, and, while it may not always be possible to *'avoid loud and aggressive persons'*, I am trying to *'take kindly the counsel of the years'*, and I do believe that *'the universe is unfolding as it should'*!

Eileen Dunne is a newscaster with RTÉ. She currently presents the Nine O'Clock News, and Classic Melodies on Lyric FM on a Sunday evening. A Dubliner, Eileen is married to the actor Macdara Ó Fátharta and they have one son, Cormac.

ADRIENNE MURPHY

Living Inspiration

UNTIL MY SON CAOIMH'S DIAGNOSIS of autism at the age of two-and-a-half, I'd been like other people who are untouched by disability. I'd found the prospect of having a child with a severe disability so terrifying that I couldn't even bring myself to contemplate it.

I believe that having a child who is very different and very vulnerable throws you into the extremes of the human condition. Profound confusion, bereavement and loss; the struggle to let go of expectations, and accept that life isn't turning out how you'd planned it; coming to terms with the demands and stresses of being a carer; the realisation that, in your case, parenting will have no cut-off point; the need to rapidly educate yourself about your child's special requirements, and to adjust your lifestyle and living conditions so as to help him as much and as quickly as you can: all of these challenges are to be expected with an autism diagnosis. What you don't expect, however – particularly in the midst of incapacitating grief – is to have to fight like a wild animal to get the means of support that your child urgently needs. And then, when you do get them, they are severely lacking. The fundraising onus on parents with autistic children is enormous in Ireland, and this presents a whole other obstacle.

Rage against the discrimination and cruelty of the state towards people like my son is one of the most difficult emotions that I've ever had to process. Today in Ireland, thousands of children and adults with autism and their families are going through living hell, not because of autism, but because of a lack of proper help and support from our society as a whole. In a very real sense, the disability and hardship that these people and their families are experiencing is artificially imposed. Loneliness, isolation and a lack of effective support are the only real disabilities.

While I was pregnant with Caoimh, I read a story in a British newspaper about a single mother who took her own life and the life of her four-year-old autistic son by jumping off a bridge into a river. I can imagine the sorrow, isolation, stress and exhaustion that drove this woman into deciding there was only one way out. For months on end sometimes, we've had to deal with extremes of behaviour in Caoimh - hour-long tantrums and violent assaults, furniture throwing, screaming fits necessitating builders' ear muffs - extremes that are unimaginable to parents of typical children. Worse than the stress for me is the sadness that the 'perpetrator' is my darling child, whose true nature is actually sweet, loving and gentle. What stops me from wanting to jump into a river during the really tough times is the huge amount of support I have from family and friends, and the expert guidance that we get from autism professionals, who are able to educate Caoimh and us as his family out of whatever current impasse we've found ourselves in.

Having a child with special needs will force you like nothing else to adopt a 'glass half-full' attitude. Are you willing to live your life seeing your beloved child as a helpless mass of disabilities and deficits, of failure to conform to the 'norm'? Or do you want to liberate yourself from the 'mind-forged manacles' of societal conditioning, and see your child as an extraordinary person with amazing potential and special gifts to bring to the world? When I started looking for and finding Caoimh's abilities rather than his disabilities, he responded immediately by leaping ahead in confidence and contentment. The challenging behaviour of people with autism – like everyone's – is a response to unmet needs. And because autistic people tend to need so much help in the areas of communication, human relationships and social interaction, learning to meet their needs brings their carers, teachers, families and friends an amazing wealth of 'insider knowledge' on what it really means to be a connected human being.

It is said that we're on this planet to learn: I believe that people with special needs are in so many ways here to teach. Because people with autism have exceptionally heightened sensory awareness, because they live so much in the moment and are often non-verbal, being with them affords us a glimpse into a parallel, 'other' world which literally shimmers with the kind of magic that you experience in a meditative state, when the fretting, incessantly chattering cognitive mind is made to shut up for a while.

I believe that embracing autism has accelerated my spiritual evolution much more than years of dedicated yoga and medi -tation ever could. But, when I have the time, I also use these techniques – yoga and meditation – to help me process what's going on. They enable me to dip into the nourishing, heal- ing, subtle energy of the soul. I also try to keep my body, mind and emotions as healthy as they can be, because I need to be at my peak to properly meet the challenges in my life. This strong awareness of and dedication to my own healing is another of Caoimh's many gifts to me. I use everything from good nutrition to shamanic counseling to bring me along the path to wholeness. Fun, socialising, love, sensuality, hedonism and excitement make me very happy. After quite a few years in the wilderness, I'm at the stage at last where I make sure I get regular doses of these.

While I believe that the purpose of life is to cultivate happi- ness, I can't stand that unrelentingly positive, 'it's all good' attitude, often spoken through clenched teeth or a trembling lower lip. Processed emotion is not the same as repressed emotion. We need to feel our feelings, no matter how fright- ening. They'll keep coming back at us until we do. A diag- nosis of severe disability in your child precipitates profound bereavement. The grief is not constant, but it is unending. Despite the joy Caoimh gives me, periodically the terrible pain comes knocking on my door. It starts as a feeling of being 'off' that day. At first I try to ignore it: an unpleasant scratch on the surface of my consciousness, an uncomfortable clothing tag that I can't be bothered to deal with right now. Then I sense the sharks begin to circle and it frightens me. I panic, ring people, get drunk, try to distract myself. Anything but face the sharks of grief. But what I'm learning is that resisting the sharks actually increases and extends my suffering and fear. I'm getting better at simply succumbing to them and letting them take me. Then I lament loudly and copiously for Caoimh's lonely predicament, for the sorrows, struggles and responsibilities that Fiach, my older son, faces as Caoimh's only sibling, and for my own losses. And, of course, the tears are a cleansing. Because letting myself feel all that pain actually helps restore my equilibrium. I presume that I will occasionally mourn like this for the rest of my life.

I paint a tough picture, but the truth is that I'm very happy much of the time, and more so now that Caoimh's early intervention is starting to pay off, and he's becoming a far more contented, less fearful, more trusting little boy.

Yet I don't think I'd ever known, before trying to cope with the extremes of Caoimh's challenging behaviour, what it really means to be left with no recourse but to fall to your knees and beg for spiritual intervention. All I can say is that it works. Here are some other thoughts that I try to remember to tell myself when I'm in crisis:

♦   You are a 'spirit being' having a human experience. In no time at all, you will be dead, everyone involved will be dead, and none of this will matter a jot any more.

◆ Observe your stress and pain and fear. Where are you watching from when you do? Detachment puts you in touch with the eternal soul, which is beyond human suffering. Remain detached and observing until this particular storm is over. It will pass.

◆ Accept what is. Resistance increases suffering. Breathe and feel. Don't think.

◆ You are being taught a fundamental lesson: that happiness is an inside job. Real happiness is not contingent on outside circumstances. It's a harsh lesson. Stop praying for your sick child for a moment. Instead pray for your own strength and endurance.

◆ Are you beating yourself up? Flood your being with self-love through your heart right now. You are exhausted. By hook or by crook, get a good night's sleep soon. You are working very hard. Work is love made manifest.

◆ Pain can be a gateway to the soul. It is possible to use this moment for rapid spiritual advancement. You can also cry, and cry, and cry.

Adrienne Murphy is a writer and journalist based in Dublin, whose work regularly appears in Hot Press *and* The Irish Times. *She also works as a freelance book editor. The mother of an autistic child, Adrienne is a well-known advocate for the rights of children with autism in Ireland. She is also an environmental campaigner.*

MICHAEL O'FLYNN

MY PHILOSOPHY IN LIFE IS TO be sincere. Treat everyone the way that you would like to be treated yourself. How we interact with others - family, friends, colleagues and strangers - is of the utmost importance. People deserve respect: none of us are worth more, and none are worth less than anyone else.

In the same way, I also strongly believe that in life and in business, people and relationships are key. If you engage positively with people, they will engage positively with you in return. How we interact with, and respond to, people shapes our rapport with them - whether this is by returning phone calls and e-mails in a timely manner, being available to offer advice or by following through on commitments made. I believe that this philosophy contributes to building strong relationships, both personal and professional, and to building a strong business.

Have the confidence to trust your own instincts. Instinct is very important and it always amazes me how often people don't follow theirs. This is one of the most valuable attributes a person has and I believe that more people should follow their gut instincts. Sometimes, people can hugely complicate simple matters, when in fact common sense and instinct is all that is required.

For me, motivation is a hunger. There is a theory that some people are born naturally motivated. Another theory suggests that motivation can be acquired. I believe that everyone has some level of motivation. Whatever level that may be, there are, of course, days where one feels less motivated, and it is then a matter of just getting on with things and moving forward. Goal setting is extremely important to motivation and to success. I am motivated by the desire to reach the goals I set. I am also motivated by mistakes I make: I believe that if we recognise our mistakes, we stand to learn more from them than from our successes.

Family is key to me and always has been. My family help me to remain positive, motivated and they are a neverending source of happiness. I also genuinely enjoy helping out where I can. Being involved with my family, friends, community and charities is something I like to do and I feel that there is an onus on everyone to give something back. I find it more rewarding to contribute than to receive, and this is a definite source of happiness for me. I also feel that the positive effects of sport and keeping fit on both body and mind cannot be recommended enough.

I believe that strong relationships exist between philosophy, motivation and happiness. If a person is fundamentally happy, it is likely that they will be more motivated. If a person has a positive philosophy on life, it is likely that they will attract happiness. It is therefore important, especially in times like these, to devote time to following a positive philosophy, to keeping motivated and to those things that make you truly happy. Everything else is secondary.

Michael O'Flynn is Chairman and Managing Director of the O'Flynn Group, one of the largest residential and construction firms in the south of Ireland; Tiger Developments, a London based property development and investment company with operations in the UK and Europe; Victoria Hall, one of the largest providers of university accommodation in the UK; and Shelbourne Senior Living, a provider of luxury, independent living for seniors in the UK. He is a Director of the Children's Medical and Research Foundation in Crumlin, a Director of the Cork University Foundation Board and a former Chairman of the Construction Industry Federation Southern Region. He is married with four children.

MARIE MURRAY

Happiness

HAPPINESS IS ELUSIVE. IT IS the state that is most desired, least defined and most difficult to attain. Even when acquired, it is not always recognised, so that it becomes apparent by its absence when it is lost. It is then that we wish that we had savoured what we had and wish we had known how lucky we were.

Happiness cannot be bought. It is least obtainable when it is actively sought. It is achieved through neither hedonism nor asceticism, particularly when gaining happiness is the goal. Happiness cannot be sold, but the belief that it can be produced, packaged and purchased is big business. It brings wealth to those who peddle promises of pleasure and it brings disappointment to those who believe that happiness can be got in this way.

Wealth does not guarantee happiness. While it may be better to be miserable in comfort than in poverty, and while there is an inevitable link between poverty and unhappiness, having wealth does not automatically mean feeling good. Research into the happiness of lottery winners, for example, shows how little having possessions contributes to contentment and how often sudden acquisition of large sums of money can bring misery to those unprepared for the altered emotional dynamics with family, friends and society that can follow.

Additionally, while most people agree with the maxim 'health is wealth', it is usually not until one's health is threatened that we appreciate health as the ultimate wealth. Perspective on life is altered radically by the loss of health so that we truly experience the grief, identified by Dante, of recalling '*a time of happiness when in misery*'.

Positive psychology supports the philosophical–theological perspective that longing for things makes us unhappy. Psychology has also attempted to identify the states, the traits, the types of people, the familial conditions, the educational experiences and the social environment most conducive to feelings of well being, of self-esteem, of optimism and of happiness. There are no guarantees from any psychotherapy model that unmitigated happiness will be the outcome; rather, to paraphrase Sigmund Freud, the endeavour is simply to turn people's utter misery into '*normal human unhappiness*'.

And this is important, for one of the major blocks to

happiness that arises clinically is the belief that young people in particular have that they are somehow psychologically deficient if they are not happy all the time and that they are personally to blame if they seek a deeper meaning than self-indulgence in their lives. This is why existentialism may reassure them that it is all right to sometimes view our world as utterly absurd and to seek to redefine ourselves within it, to sometimes march to a different tune and to wish to compose our own melody in life.

The requirement to be happy has been foisted upon us as a right, an obligation and a measure of our psychological stability, as if feelings of unhappiness are indices of psychological volatility and vulnerability. This makes the 'unhappy' feel guilty and the 'happy' feel anxious lest their current happiness be squandered or taken away. Instead, our major psychological challenge today might be to understand and tolerate the vicissitudes of life. It might be to accept that we are lucky if happiness visits sometimes, if tragedy does not strike, if we experience no more than the usual uncertainties, disappointments, losses, self-doubts and injustices that are the weave of living and of this life and if we can retain reasonable optimism when things go wrong.

The quest to discover, delineate, describe and define happiness is endless. For what is this happiness we seek? For some, it is acceptance of oneself in all one's eccentricities. It is work well done. It is adversity overcome. It is something to do, someone to love and something to hope for. It is filling the hour. It is looking forward to tomorrow. It is getting through today. It is knowing that life will be better. It is being glad that things are good.

Happiness may be matching our wants to our possessions and our ambitions to our capacities. Alternatively, it may be Michelangelo's desiring '*more than we can accomplish*', poet Robert Browning's joy in '*reaching beyond our grasp*', or writer Nathaniel Hawthorne's acceptance that happiness, like '*the butterfly we chase, is likely to alight upon us when we sit*'. For some people, happiness is music that invades the soul. It is silence. It is solitude. It is holding a new novel, or the tattered, much thumbed copy of the text we love best. It is a whole day gardening. It is sea and sky It is fishing. It is walking. It is talking. It is righting a wrong. It is unexpected affirmation. It is being accepted by a crowd.

Happiness is loving and being loved. Happiness is people. It is friends. It is in the eyes of those we care about. It is cards that wish us luck. It is exams that go okay. It is a feeling, an emotion, a belief, an idea. It is holding one's newborn or one's own child's child. It is remembering former happiness and being glad of those memories that nothing can erase. It is believing in future happiness. It is Horace's valuing the day, and '*calling the day one's own*'. It is not being emotionally anaesthetised. It is not asking if we are happy, for then it flies away.

But what is most extraordinary and significant in all the work in relation to human happiness is that the ingredients that emerge most often as being useful in our quest for happiness are optimism, altruism, gratitude, forgiveness and fulfilment. This is because happiness is a form of love. Because love is a condition in which the happiness of another is essential to our own, and research on happiness equally shows that our happiness increases when we give happiness away.

from *Living our Times* by Marie Murray, 2007

Clinical psychologist and author, Marie Murray is Director of Student Counselling Services at University College Dublin. A regular contributor to radio and print media, she is an Irish Times *health columnist.*

WILLIAM REVILLE

Our Wonderful World

SCIENCE SHOWS US THAT WE LIVE in a world that has physically organised its own development. It began almost 14 billion years ago, with a massive explosion - the big bang - at a single point of origin, and it has been expanding outwards ever since. We know how the stars formed and how the ninety-two natural elements were formed - most of them forged in stars. We humans are based on carbon and every atom of carbon in our bodies was made in a star. We know how our solar system was formed about 5 billion years ago and we know, in principle, how life began on earth over 3 billion years ago, as a simple single form. We know how life evolved from that simple form into the myriad forms of life - including ourselves - that inhabit our earth today.

We understand the four fundamental forces that determine everything physical that happens in the universe: gravity, the electromagnetic force, and the strong and the weak nuclear forces. We know about the large scale structure of the universe. And we can predict a lot about the future: we know, for example, that about 5 billion years from now, our sun will slowly die and that humanity will end, unless we have success-fully found a way to colonise another part of the universe.

Science can explain how the universe bootstrapped its way from pure energy in the beginning to me writing these words today, without any need to invoke a supernatural agency. The basic nature of matter and energy, and the laws of physics conspired to bring all of this about. And yet we must ask the question: why is the basic nature of things so fantastically fruitful? If this basic nature had been even slightly different, and it could have been, nothing very interesting would have happened at all.

Christianity teaches that we are made in the image of the creator of the world and that our purpose is to grow in wis-dom and love, before joining our creator in another dimen-sion. But, even if you are not religious in the conventional sense, science shows us a world that is sublimely creative in itself - a world that, in its development, seems to transcend the mere material, a natural world that can, nevertheless, give us a sense of the divine.

Science shows that we are all tied up in a fantastic adventure. To understand this is wonderful - to appreciate it is a blessing.

William Reville is Professor of Biochemistry, College Radiation Protection Officer and Public Awareness of Science Officer at UCC, where he has worked since 1997. He also writes the weekly 'Science Today' column in The Irish Times. *William is married with two children.*

Niamh Brennan

People will forget what you did. People will forget what you said. People will never forget how you made them feel.
Maya Angelou

WE LIVE IN A WORLD IN which it is perhaps, more than ever, impossible to escape harsh realities. Everything bad that happens is almost immediately brought to our consciousness by the instant communication systems of global electronic media. There is virtually no corner of the world that is hidden from us; there is virtually no corner of the world in which we can truly hide away.

Reality is inevitable. And, in consequence, we need a philosophy of life that faces up to reality. Each of us has to point the bow of our boat into the wave every day and in every way. Meeting this challenge requires inner strength.

That inner strength depends on seeing the good rather than the bad; on being grateful rather than resentful; on celebrating the successes and achievements of others, rather than envying them; on empathy with the problems of others rather than closing our minds and hearts to their pain.

Building that inner strength is a lifetime's work: it is a work that is never done. Doing the 'right thing' as distinct from the 'easy thing' is the exercise that brings 'inner strength'. But rectitude without altruism is sterile, lonely and futile.

That's where love comes in.

We cannot expect in life that our cups will always be overflowing. My hope is that I will always be able to see my cup as half-full rather than half-empty, that I will always be grateful for the good things that surround us and regard the bad things I encounter as reminders of just how good the good things are. I see life's journey as an opportunity to be warmed by love.

What is love? It is easier to recognise than to define. It is easier to experience than describe. But, at its heart, is identifying with the other person, sharing and empathising with their emotions and experiences: putting 'me' in the heart and mind of 'you', putting 'you' in the same place as 'me', making 'us' of 'me' and 'you'. Celebrating others, respecting others, regarding others as part of oneself.

It has been said that love is the only thing of which 'the more you give, the more you have'. It cannot be possessed or owned. That is the only 'overflowing cup' to which we can all aspire. The warmth of love: what can be better than that? Money cannot buy it. Ambition cannot possess it.

Possessions cannot substitute for it. It is all around us, but somehow cannot be grasped: it can only be felt.

Now that is some reason for optimism.

Professor Niamh Brennan, BSc (Microbiology), PhD (Warwick University), FCA, CDir, holds the Michael MacCormac Professor of Management at University College Dublin. She is also Academic Director of the Centre for Corporate Governance at UCD.

Ronan Mullen

A FEW YEARS AGO, A FRENCH friend of mine came up with a phrase that surprised me as we discussed our philosophies of life. 'I wasn't brought up in the love of God,' he said. I was struck by the tone of regret in his voice. But also touched by his generous assessment of what it means to be brought up as a Christian.

If I feel, all things considered, deeply happy, it is not because I have a particularly virtuous attitude to life or that anything very exceptional has happened to me. I just got lucky. I was fortunate to have loving parents and to be brought up on a farm where I might be required on occasion to venture into the fields at midnight to check up on a cow about to calve. Faced with an infinity of stars on a cool, crisp summer night, you have to acknowledge the deep mystery at the heart of things.

From an early age, I was invited to believe that there was a reason for it all. I learned that the things no mortal could explain could be understood in another way. That the longing for good in the heart of each person was a reminder of the good Author of all things. It wasn't a big step for me to take. The stars had taught me to wonder and to realise that there were things beyond human understanding. The humility to have faith comes easily, when your mind realises its limited potential to explain the existence of anything. Faith becomes reasonable.

Life, lit up by faith, isn't painfree. But you have a deeper interior knowledge that you are on the right track. Believing that you are not just a collection of chemicals but a beloved creature transforms the way you see yourself and others. You discover responsibilities, but responsibility backed by love and reason is never unbearable. As a politician, I try to promote the common good of believers and non-believers, in a climate where some people wrongly think that religious hope darkens, rather than lights up, human understanding. My political philosophy is simple. There can be no real conflict about what to do, if we can all agree on the awesome dignity of the human person. If we start from there, we can find the right means and rules to order our lives together. But we need to engage our hearts and our brains at the same time.

In private life, I try not to let my personal feelings become a turn-off for people who, unlike me, were not lucky enough to be 'brought up in the love of God'. I wish you all the happiness I have known. And if you care to go in search of it, I recommend a week down on the farm. But go there in the summer.

Senator Ronan Mullen is an independent senator elected to represent the National University of Ireland constituency in Seanad Éireann in 2007. He has written columns for the Irish Examiner *and the* Irish Daily Mail, *and lectures in Law, Communications and Personal Development at the Institute of Technology in Blanchardstown, Dublin.*

AIDAN STOREY

The weak can never forgive.
Forgiveness is the attribute of the strong.
                                    Mahatma Gandhi

OF ALL THE CLIENTS THAT COME to me, the ones I have the most success with are the ones who can learn to forgive, and let go of any hurt and injustice done to them. Forgiveness is not an easy thing. To forgive is to surrender, and to surrender is to admit that you have lost. It's easy to say we forgive, but the real lesson is in letting go of the hurt, pain and anger that rage within.

Prior to forgiveness, we travel through many stages of blocked feelings and emotions before we finally let go and find our true self again. Your true self wants to live in the present and be happy. The unforgiving you stays stuck in the darkness of the past and becomes bitter and negative. I know this to be true, because I myself stayed in the darkness of the past. A past where I had endured sexual abuse at a very young age by my teacher. I had buried this violent act against me so deeply, that, years later, when it did surface, I couldn't understand how and why any adult could do this to a child.

I searched and searched, but could not find the answer and I began to feel hatred in my heart, something that I'd never experienced before. I vowed never to forgive him. Eventually, I asked God and my Angels for help and so in my moments of prayer, meditation and stillness, I allowed the love and understanding of God and His Angels into my soul.

Over the course of time, They showed me how to forgive. I was angry and ashamed. The anger and shame was with myself, for allowing it to happen, and I was also very angry with the abuser. These were the emotions that flooded me, and with every emotion came terrible feelings of being deprived and unworthy. Deprived of a childhood and a normal life, and unworthy, because in some weird way I was blaming myself.

Many victims of abuse experience these types of reactions, and they are as bad, if not worse, than the abuse itself. Then come the blocks that keep you rooted in the past and prevent you from moving on. My blocks were resentment and anxiety. My resentment was my hatred for this man, and my anxiety was my fear of moving on. Being a victim had become the norm for me.

Eventually, when I pieced all these issues together, I realised I was still allowing that man and his actions to take away my power and keep me stuck in the past. So, to set myself free, I had to first forgive myself and then to forgive him. To forgive myself, I had to admit my innocence and replace my fear with courage and then move into that inner peace of love, which is God, the energy of unconditional love that lives in every one of us.

Then, it was time to deal with my abuser. I knew I had to do it or be trapped for the rest of my life in that dark energy. My forgiveness was not only about setting him free it was also about setting myself free, and cutting the chains he had placed on me many years ago, the chains of guilt, shame and darkness. So I forgave him, asking that he go in love, light and forgiveness and that he be set free, and in doing so, I asked that I be set free from the burden I carried.

I didn't feel instantly at peace after doing this forgiveness ceremony. I found I had to repeat it again and again over time before I felt that I had let go. Forgiveness shows that we can separate the person from the bad action, but that does not mean condoning in any way the evil they do. Shortly after I had forgiven the man in question, my Angel came to me and spoke these words that I will never forget, 'You are no longer a victim. You are now victorious. In forgiveness, you have allowed a new chapter of your life to begin and given yourself permission to move on.'

If, daily, we try and forgive the petty little things in our lives - the sharp word, the personal insult, being ignored and put down by people - bitterness no longer eats us up inside. When we practise letting go, we are preparing for, and ready to give, true forgiveness when we really have to.

Forgiveness is not about letting go of the memory: it's about letting go of the pain.

Aidan Storey is one of Ireland's most well-known spiritual healers. He sees and receives messages from Angels. His book, Angels of Divine Light, *will be published in October 2009.*

DAVID COLEMAN

WHEN I WASH MY CAR, I take great care. I can hear the words of my father echoing, 'If a job is worth doing, it is worth doing well.' Then I get an offer of help from one or all of my three children. Suddenly, I have no control over the 'cleaning'. Well-intentioned smears appear where clean bodywork had been moments before. I don't always like the way they choose to clean. If I'm honest, my first thought is to shout at them that I'll do it myself, because then I will do it right, to my own exacting standards.

Sometimes, I don't have the patience, and I do shout at them. When I can manage to hold back, it is only with the greatest difficulty. I grit my teeth and try to be encouraging of their efforts to help. I know I struggle in this scenario because I am a bit of a control freak.

I have also learned, however, that, just like any other parent, I have to let go. If I make every decision for my children, they will never learn how to make good decisions for themselves. If they are never allowed to make mistakes, they will lose opportunities to learn. If I rule their lives now, always on my terms, how will they know what they want to achieve in their own lives later?

Many of us rue the lack of motivation of our teenagers. They seem to have no internal drive and they seem to be resistant to being externally motivated by the promise of reward or the threat of consequence. But when they were younger, what opportunities did we give them to inspire us with their creativity or try it their way?

If parenting is worth doing, it is worth doing well.

David Coleman is a clinical psychologist. Most recently, he has become well known for his work on television on the popular RTÉ shows, Families in Trouble, *and* Teens in the Wild. *David is the author of* Parenting is Child's Play: How to Give Your Child the Best Start in Life and Have Fun Doing It, *as well as being a regular contributor to radio and print media. David also lectures around the country on parenting issues.*

MARY FITZGERALD

BLACK KITTEN HEELS WITH POINTY TOES. Size five. Even now, more than four years after grim-faced Jordanian police officers waved me through the security cordon, it is the image of that pair of shoes that remains vivid. Amid the blood-soaked linen tablecloths and the wilting remains of bridal bouquets ground into the carpet by screaming, panicking guests, the sight of such a dainty pair of shoes begged so many questions. Had the owner survived the blast that had ripped through the wedding reception when a suicide bomber detonated the belt of explosives packed around his waist? Or was she among the dead?

Being a journalist can often feel both a privilege and a burden. The privilege comes from having firsthand access to the events that help shape the contours of history. But that can often involve having to trespass on the most harrowing moments of people's lives. The stories of so many linger with me, continuing to move and often inspire me long after I have packed my notebook away, but few more enduringly than that of Nadia and Ashraf, the couple whose new life together was so cruelly disrupted that cold November evening.

I met Ashraf, wide-eyed and pale with shock, in the emergency unit of one of Amman's largest hospitals, just hours after the suicide bombing that claimed the lives of twenty-seven of his wedding guests, among them his father and both Nadia's parents. I met Nadia some days later, and what began as a series of interviews soon deepened into friendship. Maybe it had something to do with the fact we were both in our twenties and would most likely have become friends if our paths had crossed in less tragic circumstances. Perhaps it had something to do with the way Nadia talked about her unspeakable loss, and how it chimed with my own grief over losing my father to cancer three years before. We laughed and cried together; we watched the video of the couple's engagement party over and over again, as Nadia pointed out the friends and family members that had died at her wedding; we joked around with Nadia's nephew, an adorable little boy too young to fully comprehend what had befallen his family.

Nadia was twenty-four when she lost her mother and father, on what was supposed to be the happiest day of her life. Her remarkable strength, courage and serenity in the face of such horror never ceases to amaze and inspire me. After experiencing what would have propelled so many others into the depths of despair or hatred, Nadia and Ashraf instead drew on their love for each other as an antidote to the grief that could so easily have consumed them. Today they have a daughter, named after Nadia's mother Hala, and the e-mails Nadia sends me detail a family life that has carved joy out of tragedy and hope out of darkness.

I never did find out who owned that pair of women's shoes, or what had happened to her that night, but the story of Nadia and Ashraf, and how their love triumphed over the most terrible loss, will stay with me forever.

Mary Fitzgerald is the Irish Times' *award-winning Foreign Affairs Correspondent. She has worked across the Middle East, Africa and South Asia, reporting from more than twenty countries, including Egypt, Syria, Lebanon, Saudi Arabia, Sudan, Pakistan and Afghanistan. She takes a particular interest in issues pertaining to globalisation, development and the Islamic world.*

Tom Doorley

THE PROSAIC REASON FOR GETTING OUT of bed in the mornings is the pressing need to make a living and to provide for my family. Prosaic as this may be, I still think it's reasonably noble. The advantage for me in doing a number of jobs (writing for both newspapers and for advertising; consulting on wine; working in broadcasting) is that I can avoid boredom and routine.

Love is what makes life worth living. Do almost anything with love, and it has a certain validity. I like the Quaker notion of there being 'a God in everyone' – whatever God may be. I'm a kind of pantheist, I suppose. Taking pleasure in growing things, especially food, and in landscapes, particularly the gentle topography of East Cork and West Waterford, and in the company of friends and loved ones: this is what makes me tick. There's a thin line, I suppose, between enjoying simple things and being shallow, but watching a summer sunset from our terrace is enough to make me feel at one with the world. I also enjoy creating something out of nothing, which is the definition of writing.

I am sceptical about certainty. It excludes wonder. Making sense of the world is more than a life's work, and I envy the ability of small children to live intensely in the present. The present is all that we have. Regrets and hopes aside, I believe in the maxim, carpe diem. Seize the day and do it now, if you possibly can.

Tom Doorley is a writer and broadcaster with particular interests in food, wine and gardening. He lives with his wife Johann and their three daughters on a hillside that straddles the border between Cork and Waterford. Tom writes a weekly column for The Irish Times.

Bishop Wille Walsh

Philosophy for Living: A Work in Progress

I GREW UP IN A RURAL community in North Tipperary in the middle of the last century. Nobody whom I knew had a 'philosophy for living'. They just lived. Crops were sown and harvested, cows were milked, hay was saved and God was in the heavens. There were no 'bad people' around, though Christy Ring and a certain politician were not exactly favourites in my home! There was, of course, a bad war going on, but that was over there somewhere in Europe. We went to Mass on Sunday, said the rosary at night and feared God.

I went to boarding school in St Flannan's College in Ennis, where rules were strict, food was basic and discipline was sometimes severe. Hurling was the escape from that harsher side of boarding school life. Priests came to speak to us about vocations and, in 1952, of fifty-five of us who sat the Leaving Certificate, some twenty went to study for priesthood the following September. I have often asked myself, why did I go? I think my motive was the belief that it was the only way I could save my soul – not exactly a noble motive and not at all one that would satisfy me today.

'Philosophy for living'? Well, we began with the study of philosophy in the seminary, but I never saw it as having anything to do with life. And yet there was a 'philosophy for living' emerging. I think I began to develop a philosophy rooted more in the example and teaching of Jesus Christ, rather than one based on any strict following of rules and regulations of the Church. After three years' study in Maynooth, I was lucky enough to be sent to Rome and was exposed to the Italian philosophy for living expressed in the wave of the hands, the shrugging of shoulders and the, 'I be *cattolico – cattolico, ma non fanatico.*' I am grateful for those years in Rome which freed me somewhat from the oppressive and fear-fuelled style of religion in the Ireland of that era.

My life as a priest has consisted in twenty-five years teaching in a boys' secondary school, seven years in a parish, fourteen years as a bishop, all the time developing a 'philosophy for living'. The teaching came relatively easy to me, and was always enjoyable. I suppose the students kept me generally alive. The angry young men of the 1960s who were in a hurry to change the world resonated with me and many young priests who were colleagues, as we were in a hurry to change the Church. Pope John XXIII and Vatican II raised our hopes, but the publication of *Humanae Vitae* dampened our expectations of rapid change.

My 'philosophy for living' continued to develop with more and more emphasis on the example and teachings of Jesus Christ. I believe that I became more concerned about the values of justice and peace, of forgiveness and compassion, and of friendship and love, and less concerned about the rules and regulations of our Church. Working with married lay-people in the areas of marriage preparation and the counselling of marriages in difficulties, I became less judgemental and more aware of the goodness of people and the awful struggle that life can be for some.

Working in a parish gave me a new insight into the lives of the sick and the elderly, and taught me to thank the Lord for my good fortune in relation to health. Being in regular contact with elderly people was a new experience after the years of teaching. Some of them gave me new and valuable insights through their own 'philosophies for living'.

When I was appointed bishop in 1994, I took as my motto 'Cineáltas Chríost', meaning 'the kindliness of Christ'. Perhaps that was an effort to put words to a 'philosophy for living'. Obviously, I am very conscious that I regularly fail to live up that ideal.

Life as bishop for the past fourteen years has been very fulfilling and life-giving, except for the dreadful area of child sexual abuse. Trying to deal appropriately with this has been a real nightmare. Listening to the pain of victims of abuse has to be one of the most heartrending experiences in life. And, indeed, asking a priest colleague to stand aside because of an allegation of abuse is also heartrending. And dare one say that abusers are not the monsters we sometimes paint them, but broken human beings who, for some strange reason, often from experiences in their own childhood, have not matured in the area of sexuality? And you thank God that you have managed your own struggle with sexuality and celibacy, that at least it hasn't been destructive, even if at times it has been a difficult struggle.

And the struggle to live out the 'Cinéaltas Chríost' philosophy of life goes on. May the kindliness of Christ – 'Cinéaltas Chríost' – always surround you, gentle reader.

Bishop Willie Walsh, a native of Roscrea, was ordained in Rome in 1959. He spent twenty-five years teaching in St Flannan's College, Ennis. He worked for a time as a curate in Ennis before being ordained as Bishop of Killaloe in 1994. A strong advocate for marginalised groups, especially Travellers, he is a frequent contributor to the media. He has pursued a lifelong interest in hurling, and has been involved in coaching teams at parish, college and county levels.

JOHN WATERS

LOOKING BACK NOW, I CANNOT RECALL a single moment of epiphany, when I understood, even briefly, the enormity of what I now understand religion to signify. But I have a sense today, acquired several eventful decades later, that I never recall having had as a child, of what religion is, and what it might offer. The strange thing is that I always had this sense, except that I never thought of it as religion. I had, as a child, an acute sense that religion might be important, but no sense of what its content might be. I was aware of the things I now think of religion as containing, but had no idea that these could be called religion.

It was many, many years later that I awoke one morning with a phrase running around my head and, in the background, the sound of a wind swirling through trees, and realised that I had had as a child the most vibrant sense of the religious ... The book was *The Religious Sense*, in which Fr Luigi Giussani, by telling us what religion is, implicitly tells us what religion is not:

Picture yourself being born, coming out of your mother's womb at the age you are now at this very moment in terms of your development and consciousness. What would be the first, absolutely your initial reaction? If I were to open my eyes for the first time in this instant, emerging from my mother's womb, I would be overpowered by the wonder and awe of things as a 'presence'. I would be bowled over and amazed by the stupefying repercussion of a presence which is expressed in current language by the word 'thing'. Things! That's 'something'! 'Thing', which is a concrete and, if you please, banal version of the word 'being'. Being: not as some abstract entity but as presence, a presence which I do not myself make, which I find. A presence which imposes itself on me.

from *Lapsed Agnostic* by John Waters, 2008

John Waters is a newspaper columnist and author. Lapsed Agnostic is his most recently published book.

JOHN CREEDON

THE FIRST OF MY FOUR GIRLS was born when I was twenty years old. At the time I was buffing floors at the local Pennys store for money. It was 1980s Cork and it was all about trying to make ends meet. Now the eldest of my girls is about to get married and I find myself entering a new phase of my time on this planet. I was always curious about life, nature and the human condition, but now that the girls are virtually up-and-running, I'm looking forward to having more time for silence and a little 'non-thinking'. The mind can be a relentless taskmaster, and needs to be stilled from time to time, lest we begin to think that we are our minds!

Words can be very cumbersome and often serve us very badly. For example, if I tell you that I've just seen a bird in a tree, you are likely to nod in agreement as if you understand what I mean. Yet you may be visualising a blackbird on an oak tree, while I actually saw a robin in a holly bush. Similarly, everyone's concept of 'God' is different. I mean, both Bush and bin Laden invoke 'God'! I think they've both missed the point. It sounds like both men suffer from a very similar attachment to ideology. As they say in Tibet, 'He who claims he knows, claims. He who knows, knows.'

In that regard, I would aspire to the Buddhist pursuit of non-attachment. At the end of the day, no one has been there and back, so noone knows the mystery of life. And, as the song goes: '*I think I'll just let the mystery be.*'

I feel we are all pilgrims. Even those of us who are not members of a Church are still trying to get to a place where it doesn't hurt anymore. More often than not, though, we are likely to reach for pleasure rather than happiness. The human race has been mixing up those two for millennia. In these times, we are offered all sorts of painkillers and distractions from the melancholy of the human condition: drink, dope, entertainment, twenty-four-hour shopping. In the case of the latter, I try not to shop on Sundays. I understand that some people have no choice, so I'm not campaigning for other people to follow suit. I'm too busy trying to get my life in order to have time to save the world!

Nature for me is the portal to the sacred place. I live in the middle of the city, but I'm surrounded by nature: birds in bushes, people and their dogs, insects, little boys at football matches, the weather – the magic is everywhere! And the wilder places of west Cork are soothing to the eye and to the mind. My first glimpse of the Atlantic on the journey west, or my first footfall into a broadleaf forest – and the RTÉ mast, my career, the ESB bill are all forgotten. My life is tiny in comparison to the Atlantic.

The afterlife?

At a primary level, I feel that I'm a body and a mind, but I'm also something else – a third dimension, the observer, the one who sees my body and my mind. My body has been changing from the day I was born and so, too, has my mind. I mean, I don't inhabit the same body as I did when I was eleven years old. Nor is my mind the same. The eleven-year-old John Creedon didn't like girls and didn't shave. He had two parents and no immediate thoughts of starting a family! Whereas I am now a parent and an orphan. I have also come to notice the beauty of women! So, would the real John Creedon please stand up? That's it: I feel I'm truly neither my body nor my mind. I am the observer, the one who has witnessed the changing body and mind of John Creedon. This consciousness is, I feel, eternal. Just as energy can be neither created nor destroyed, only trans-formed, I believe that when my body and mind close down after I have drawn my last breath, my immortal energy will leave my body and return to Love.

So the times when I mess up, and they're all too frequent, I have to learn to forgive myself. I have to see that I am evolv-ing all the time and that I am not the same as I was yesterday and that I will be different again tomorrow. That's where the third dimension comes in – my spirit takes me to a place where I can forgive myself and others. I can see, from that place, that poor old John, for all his insecurities, is doing his very best.

Although I feel no need to subscribe to an institutional

Church or off-the-peg philosophy, I can see the wisdom in much religious practice. I mean, anyone who says the rosary or meditates is effectively doing what others attempt to do when walking in nature: to pass through the 'boredom portal' to a place of 'unthinking', where the mind is silenced to allow space for grace to flow and healing to take place. Didn't Jesus once say: '*Be still and know that I am God*'? I reckon the purpose of meditation, like the rosary, is just that: to still the mind and feel the universal love that flows through everything, including even the most wicked of us. No one is beyond redemption.

I love the Cambodian definition of a true philosopher. This states that the great religions are like mountains – big, immovable seats of wisdom, but still finite. They reach a point where, for all their ancient majesty, they peak and go no farther. The true pilgrim is like an individual mountain stream, beginning life on one mountain but restlessly searching for home. On its life journey, the stream passes through the other great mountains, or religions, gathering nutrients as it goes, until eventually, at journey's end, it surrenders to the ocean, rejoining the greater consciousness before precipitation takes place and it is reborn as rainfall, to begin its journey again.

I don't claim to understand the meaning of life or have all the answers. So I hope I don't sound evangelical about my beliefs, because that's all they are, beliefs. No one actually knows. I can only tell you what I feel, and in the true spirit of detachment, I reserve the right to change my mind completely tomorrow! If my beliefs are a source of annoyance to some people who read this, all I can offer them is my love – even the cranky ones!

John Creedon is a radio and television broadcaster, currently presenting RTÉ Radio 1's Late Date. He is also a columnist with the Irish Examiner, *and has toured on the Irish stand-up comedy circuit, as well as starring in the hit television comedy, Killinaskully. John is currently back at UCC studying Gaeilge Labhartha (spoken Irish), as well as learning traditional flute at Cork School of Music.*

Ronan McNulty

When I, my brothers and sister were young, we used to pass the time on interminable car journeys by playing a game. It was called, 'Why is the Sky Blue?', and we would commence by asking our parents this question, as an opening assault on their knowledge. They knew exactly what this would precipitate, but stalwartly played along, offering an answer such as, 'Because the sun is shining.' To which our cumulative wit would reply: 'But why is the sun shining?' And when my parents would attempt to parry with something like: 'Because the sun is very hot', it wasn't long before we delivered the next thrust: 'But why is the sun so hot?' And so it continued!

The great attraction of initiating this game is that you can't lose, which is precisely the type of game that children like – particularly if it means beating their omnipotent parents.

There were two possible outcomes to this game. Either, having exhausted our parents' patience, we were told to keep quiet – but we could rejoice in the moral high ground of 'those that seek the truth'. More often, however, the game would end with the answer which is not an answer – the truism: 'Because it is!', with which no further questioning was logically possible. We had reached the end of knowledge or, for the irritating children involved, shown that our parents did not, in fact, know everything.

It should be pointed out that this same game can be played to sophistic advantage with school teachers or even university professors. However, played with sincerity, it opens the door to understanding and new knowledge. Played with questions to which noone yet has answers, it underpins the process of scientific research. The farther one can progress down the chain of questions and answers, the closer one gets to the fundamental truths.

My subject, particle physics, deals with one of the most fundamental questions it is possible to ask, 'Of what is our universe made?' It is a question of great simplicity that can equally be asked by young children or ancient Greek philosophers. We work with the conceit that if we know the smallest possible constituents of nature and how they behave, then we can 'explain' the whole universe, from its initiation at the Big Bang until today, and onwards into the future.

Subjecting our world to a litany of questions inevitably leads us towards fundamental truths, often revealing beautiful connections between seemingly disparate phenomena.

For example, just as James Clerk Maxwell showed that electricity and magnetism were one and the same thing, CERN – the European Organisation for Nuclear Research –

discovered, in 1983, a particle that showed that electricity, magnetism and radioactivity are all different manifestations of the one force. Today, we are looking for a fundamental particle that answers the apparently childlike question, 'Why are things heavy?'

But for all our impressive advances, we are, and I think will always remain, caught in the dilemma that my parents were in. We will always come up against the boundaries of knowledge, and have to admit that something is the way it is, 'Because it is!'. And even were we one day to refine our knowledge to a single fundamental truth, the small child in the back of the car would merely need to ask why that truth was so, to show us both the beauty and the fallacy of our eternal search for knowledge.

Ronan McNulty obtained a BSc from UCD in Experimental and Mathematical Physics, and was awarded a PhD in Particle Physics from the University of Liverpool in 1993. He spent nine years at CERN investigating the physics of the tau lepton and bottom quark using the DELPHI detector at the Large Electron Positron Collider (LEP), before moving to Fermilab, near Chicago, where he worked on the CDF experiment at the Tevatron collider. Ronan returned to Ireland in 2003 to help found the only experimental particle physics research group in the country.

COMPASSION

In this chapter are some of the most inspiring contributions I received in the compilation of this book. These pieces are the 'art' of happiness. They are not just words: they are the actions behind the words. Day after day, year after year, such actions will inspire happiness and joy in the givers and the receivers.

The contributors show that words alone mean very little. What matters is action, not just thoughts. All of us, despite our weaknesses and our competing priorities, have the power to contribute, to be compassionate, and to make a small difference in the lives of those who need us, and an enormous difference in our own personal wealth of happiness.

In the words of Mike Meegan, showing others compassion and respect has the power to transform: '*When we treat man as he is, we make him worse than he is; when we treat him as if he already was what he potentially could be, we make him what he should be.*'

Sr Nirmala Maria

Happiness: the Joy of Loving

FROM TIME TO TIME, PEOPLE ASK US: 'What is the secret of the joy of the Missionaries of Charity?' Aware of the demands and sacrifices entailed in a life of loving and dedicated service to God, in serving Him through serving the poorest of the poor, they wonder and are attracted by our joy. St Augustine, after a long search for happiness, exclaimed when he found God: '*Late it was that I loved You, beauty so ancient and so new, late I loved You! And look, You were within me and I was outside.*' He came to understand that, '*our hearts are restless until they rest in Thee*'.

I like to think that man has a 'thirst' and, at the centre of this thirst, is an insatiable desire for happiness. Happiness for us is a necessity and strength, even physically. A deep, interior happiness expresses itself as cheerfulness, cheerfulness in the face, in the eyes, in the smile and in the warm greeting.

Some people feel that happiness means living a carefree life. But we have discovered that a life built on trust in God's infinite wisdom and unfailing love brings for us a deep peace and inner joy, in spite of trials and difficulties. Those who teach us most about happiness are the poor we meet and serve. Being poor, they experience any sign of goodness as a gift: their eyes light up on seeing the sisters, and the children run to them with ready smiles of joy. '*Blessed are the poor in spirit, for theirs is the Kingdom of God*'. (Matthew 5:3).

We hunger for love because we were made to love and be loved. God is love and He thirsts to love us and to be loved in return.

When these two thirsts meet - God's and ours - there is a surrender in love and a satiating of love. There is a resting in the Beloved as well as an energy which pushes one out in self-gift.

We express this in our fourth vow of Wholehearted and Free Services to the Poorest of the Poor. With them, we share the happiness that springs from a heart that is full of God. The more we are empty of self, the more we can share Him, His love, His presence, His compassion. The deeper our faith, the more we can see Jesus, love Jesus and serve Jesus in His distressing disguise in the poor, and in each other.

Our dearest Mother Blessed Teresa of Calcutta used to say, 'Learn to pray, for prayer enlarges the heart until it is capable of containing God's gift of Himself.' For the fruit of silence is prayer, the fruit of prayer is faith, the fruit of faith is love and the fruit of love is service, and the fruit of service is peace. Mother Teresa's message to all was, '*Keep the joy of loving Jesus in your hearts and share that joy with all you meet.*'

Sr Nirmala, born in Co. Donegal, is a nun with the Missionaries of Charity, Calcutta, the order founded by Mother Teresa.

Br Kevin Crowley

*Inspired by the spirit of St Francis of Assisi, we at the Capuchin
Day Centre welcome people in need of food, aid, who have no
home or are socially excluded and, respecting their dignity, provide
a caring, pastoral, holistic and non-judgemental service,
responsive to their needs.*

from the Mission Statement of the
Capuchin Day Centre

Apart from my parents, who worked hard all their lives and
sacrificed all they had for their children, the most powerful role
model in my life was a man who lived and died over eight centuries ago. Francis of Assisi, known and loved as 'The Father of
the Poor', left nothing to his followers in earthly goods, but
what a spiritual and social justice legacy he left behind! What
a man – what an act to follow! Francis was a practical man who
responded to the needs of the people of his time, particularly
those left behind by the rest of society, and it was in this spirit
that the Capuchin Day Centre was founded.

Those of us old enough to remember the end of the 'swinging sixties' will know that, while most of the Dublin's inner

city was thriving, some people were having difficulties coping with life and many became homeless or had to live in
hostels. Each day, a number of people came to the friary door
in Church Street, looking for food and some would gather at
the back of the church for heat, or to keep out of the rain.
The Capuchin Order felt that this was an undignified way for
people to spend their time, and so the Day Centre was
founded. From very humble beginnings, offering soup and
sandwiches to about fifty people, the centre is recognised
today as one of the biggest food services in the city, provid-
ing up to 500 meals a day, grocery parcels for people who
find it difficult to manage on social-welfare benefits, a
medical service, shower facilities and other day-care activities. It is with a great sense of gratitude to God that, through
the goodness of so many people, the centre has become a
place of hospitality and refuge for people who have been left
behind during the boom of the Celtic Tiger and whose
everyday reality has never been other than recession.

My sadness is the untimely deaths of many homeless friends
over the years, some of whom died alone on the side of the
road without anyone to care for them. I'm sure that Jesus and
His blessed Mother welcomed them with great love and that
they now enjoy what they did not have on earth: a home
where they are loved and respected.

My joy is in seeing the unbelievable generosity and kindness
of people who have kept this lifeline for the homeless in
operation for the past forty years. People today, particularly

young people, are just as generous and kind as they have ever been, and I rejoice in that.

My inspiration comes from the people who come to the centre. Just think how much courage it takes to face another day, for someone who has slept rough the night before and does not know if they will have a bed to sleep in tonight. How do they keep going? Think of the parents who want exactly the same good lives for their children as everyone else, but who simply do not have the money to provide it.

My dream for the future is that, one day, there will be no need for such a service as the Day Centre, and that everyone will have the social and financial resources to live life to the full, as God intended.

My prayers are for a world where:

♦ Everyone is treated with equal dignity and respect, as God intended

♦ The weak are protected, and no one goes hungry or poor

♦ The riches of creation are shared, and everyone can enjoy them

♦ Different races and cultures live in harmony and mutual respect

♦ Everyone works for lasting peace with true justice

♦ People will have the courage to defend the rights of those who are oppressed and powerless, and will not be afraid to face the anger and might of the powerful.

Blessing of St Francis of Assisi

May the Lord bless you and keep you.
May He show His face to you
And have mercy on you.
May He turn His countenance to you
And give you peace.

Br Kevin was born in Kilcoman, Enniskeane in west Cork in 1935. He was one of a family of five children and entered the Capuchin Franciscan Order in 1958. He was assigned to the Capuchin Friary in Church Street, Dublin, in the 1960s and founded the Capuchin Day Centre in 1969.

FR PETER MCVERRY

MANY YOUNG PEOPLE INVOLVED IN CRIME give up such activities in their early twenties. The reason: they fall in love or have a child. For the first time in their life, they have a reason not to go to jail: namely, that there is someone in their life to whom they have a unique contribution to make. In giving, their lives are transformed.

Our dignity, and our happiness, depends on our giving, not getting. Happiness defies all the laws of nature: the more you give it away, the more you have of it. A young boy and girl, madly in love, embracing each other, would not swap that moment of loving and being loved for all the goods in the world. They wish that moment would never end – surely that will be our experience in eternity? Giving brings its own rewards.

This world is such an unfair place. So many suffer so much, through no fault of their own. What can match the pain of a parent who watches their child suffer, powerless to do anything about it? What can match the gratitude of a parent to the stranger who rescues their child from certain danger? To take some little bit of that suffering from the shoulders of another human being, to bring a little more joy to someone's life, that is our purpose in life, that is why we exist, that is what makes our own lives worthwhile. In reaching out, we discover meaning.

What can match the joy of a parent who sees their child's eyes light up when they open the present the parent has given them? What can match a child's hug, expressing gratitude and love to their parent? What can match the joy of bringing happiness to the one we love? In giving, we receive so much.

Fr Peter McVerry SJ (Society of Jesus) was ordained as a Jesuit priest in 1975. Shortly after this, while working as a priest in inner-city Dublin, he encountered some homeless children and opened a hostel for them in 1979. He subsequently opened three more hostels, a residential drug detoxification centre, and two drug-free aftercare houses. He has written on many issues relating to young, homeless people, such as accommodation, drugs, juvenile justice, the gardaí, the prisons and education. In 2003, Fr McVerry produced a book of his own writings, entitled The Meaning is in the Shadows. *His most recent publication is* Jesus: Social Revolutionary?.

JOHN O'SHEA

NOTHING COULD BE MORE INSPIRING THAN the courage and ingenuity exhibited by the poorest people on the planet in their efforts to survive on a daily basis.

The sacrifices they make to feed their children; the miles travelled in punishing heat to fetch water; the patient queuing without complaint in the burning sun for a meagre pittance for which they are so grateful. These are the acts that can lift the spirit.

The bravery to meet the struggle on a daily basis, while caught in the cruel, vice-like grip of governments in other countries who don't give a damn about them, and governments in the developing world, who are entirely indifferent to their plight, takes a degree of guts that has to be seen to be appreciated.

Anyone who has witnessed this bruising battle to protect such lives that are always hanging by a thread; anyone who has seen the light in the faces and the brightness of the smiles, despite being dealt such a kick in the head, could not fail to be affected. If their hope in the face of such overwhelming tragedies – the lost children, the sickness, the hunger, if their strength does not inspire you, then really nothing will.

But I am also greatly moved by 'GOALies' (those who work with and for GOAL, our international humanitarian agency). The nurses, doctors, accountants, logisticians and others, who once upon a time only came from Ireland, but who now hail from all over the world. Their sacrifices are also inspirational. Giving up their time and their comforts to live in mosquito-infested corners of the world. Their readiness to lend their expertise and love so freely to the poorest of the poor reflects so well on this and other countries. Their example motivates people like myself.

What is my philosophy? I'm utterly convinced that we must alleviate the suffering of the poorest of the poor whenever we can. Those of us, who have and know, have an imperative to reach out to those in greatest need. Perhaps the most potent belief is that every human being has the right to enjoy, at the very least, the basics that this planet has to offer. If we can arrive at a situation where the most important issue is the survival of all people, what a journey that would have been.

John O'Shea is a former sports journalist with the (now defunct) Evening Press. He founded the international humanitarian agency, GOAL, in 1977. Since then, GOAL has spent in excess of €550 million, bringing a measure of relief to some of the world's poorest and most deprived people in almost fifty countries. John worked as a volunteer CEO with the agency until 1992, when he quit full-time journalism to concentrate all of his energy on GOAL activity.

Br Shawn Conrad O'Connor

LOVE IS THE ONLY THING THAT gives any meaning to life. Life is love, and, without love, it is simply existence. There may be fleeting pleasures, superficial excitement and adventure, but only this satisfies completely: to be loved and to love in return. I don't necessarily mean romantic love, but the purest aspect of love, one that gives itself totally to another, without counting the cost or looking for anything in return. It is a love which lays down its life for another.

I first became aware of this the moment I realised that God was real, that He was my true father, that He became a man in Jesus Christ and laid down His life for me, and that He not only loves me unconditionally, but is love itself. In an instant, I knew this as surely as I've ever known anything, and wanted nothing more than to give love back: to God first and then to all others. I knew I had to give my life over completely to Him and unite my will with His, if I was to attain lasting peace and joy in my life.

It was for this reason that I left a teaching career to become a religious brother with the Franciscan Friars of the

Renewal. Their love for God, the Catholic Church and the poor, along with a desire to spread the gospel, resonated deeply in my heart. It was a lifestyle that followed in the footsteps of St Francis of Assisi, who observed the gospel as closely as possible, radically choosing to take Christ at his word when he said: '*Go sell everything that you have and give to the poor, and you will have treasure in Heaven. Then follow me.*' (Mark 10:21).

Obviously, attempting to do this is not easy, and is never done perfectly, but trying to do it sincerely helps me to grow closer to God, and has given me a peace and fulfilment that I did not find in the world. It is a peace which lasts, and not only for this lifetime, but forever. I can't prove this, but I believe it completely. It is this belief that sustains me in the present and gives me real hope for the future, a hope for all eternity.

Br Shawn Conrad O'Connor is a member of the Franciscan Friars of the Renewal, a Roman Catholic religious order. A native of New York, he lives at St Patrick's Friary in Moyross, Limerick.

Fr Aidan Troy

FOR THREE MONTHS IN 2001, I walked with children and their parents to Holy Cross Girls' School in Belfast in the midst of the most awful violence and abuse. I learned so much. In the parents and teachers, I saw ordinary people act in an extra-ordinarily dignified way. Most of all, I saw children during those three months teach us adults not to become bitter, spiteful, hateful or sectarian. The day the protest was suspended for good, one child, when asked did she hate the protesters, simply said, 'No.' For the first time, I knew why Christ took a child and not an adult as the model of the Kingdom of God. Those little children altered me more in three months than had my previous thirty-five years as a priest put together. Sometimes, we may miss the closeness and power of people, especially children, around us.

There are families who have been to hell and back when the knock comes to their door to say that their child has died by suicide. The lights go out. The talking stops. The issue becomes getting through the next few hours. The night can be the worse because it too is dark. God is absent. In one family, the knock came twice in one month. Two sons were now dead by suicide. How do people go on living after that?

Honestly, I don't know. But they do, and one source of enormous strength is from those who have been numbed by the same news when the knock came to their own door. Bereaved and broken themselves, they come to people who are now starting that unimaginably difficult road without their loved one. They offer hope, when despair is all around. They offer strength, when absolute weakness is what is felt. They offer generously out of their own experience of despair and weakness. I want to kiss the ground these people walk on because it is holy ground. They are the unrecognised heroes and saints in our midst.

Fr Aidan Troy was born in 1945 in Bray, Co. Wicklow. He studied at UCD and Clonliffe College, prior to ordination in 1970. He served twice as Passionist Provincial in the 1980s and, for six years, in Rome as part of the General Council. He was parish priest of Holy Cross, Ardoyne, Belfast, from 2001-2008. He is now serving the English-speaking Parish of St Joseph in Paris, France. He has published one book: Holy Cross: A Personal Experience.

HARRY KENNEDY

Saigon, Sophistication and Christina Noble

IN DUBLIN IN THE 1960S, I had a primary school teacher who described pupils with long hair, brightly coloured clothes or similar as 'sophisticated'. She could make this sound like a felony. According to the Greek philosophers, sophistication consists of travelling from place to place and learning that things are done differently elsewhere. Perhaps it's because sophistication has a negative connotation in Ireland that a lot of people don't go in for it, and the media mock public servants who travel. When I was a student in the 1970s, my friends spent summers in Boston and Botswana, while I spent several summers measuring magnesium in white blood cells. This did not make me sophisticated. So now, I habitually stop in out-of-the-way places on the way home from medical conferences abroad (at my own expense, I hasten to add).

I once found myself on the side of a boulevard in Saigon, unable to get across the floods of scooters that were passing by the thousand. A policeman, seeing my difficulty, came up to my shoulder, took me by the elbow and launched us across the torrent of two-stroke engines. They simply flowed around us, as if we were swimming through a shoal of fish. Later, I found the only Irish bar in Saigon, where the owner was arguing with a less likeable policeman over the amount of his weekly contribution to the policeman's personal funds. The bar was full of ex-pat Irish engineers, there to install mobile phone networks, hydroelectric plants and the like. Through them, I got an invitation to visit the Christina Noble foundation the next day.

The children's home and clinic is in a slightly quieter part of the city, staffed by businesslike young health professionals and volunteers from all over the world, clear-eyed and idealistic. The clinic is serene, full of toys and white-tiled spaces, hospital cots and airy balconies to cool the humid days.

Vietnam is a magical place. I went to visit the tunnels of Cu Chi, where tourists can have a go at firing AK-47s (I hit the target!). On the way back, I stopped at the Cao Dai Holy See, a mix of every eastern and western religion, with the emphasis very much on dressing up and parading. Driving through the countryside, I saw water buffalo up to their shoulders in village mud ponds, and girls in traditional white silks holding on to their conical hats and sitting side-saddle on the back of the ubiquitous scooters. There were no bomb craters visible, no mangled 'copters or military trophies. Just a yellow sunset over the paddy fields.

In the 1960s and 1970s, Vietnam had a very different, unsophisticated meaning. I wish my primary teacher had been there. She would have been fascinated by the Christina

Noble foundation, by the children who are only superficially different from Irish children, and by the volunteers, all of them innocent, principled, self-sacrificing sophisticates.

Professor Harry Kennedy is a forensic psychiatrist and the Clinical Director of the Central Mental Hospital in Dublin. He qualified in Medicine in UCD in 1980, had postgraduate training in Medicine and Psychiatry, and worked in London until 2000. He distracts himself by seeing patients, concentrating on epidemiological and medico-legal research, and playing loud music.

DAVIDA DE LA HARPE

Spending time with others, and learning how they see their world is the way that, over the years, I have kept my enthusiam and love for the work and life I have. I do not give up easily on my own goals and like to think I also give real support to family and friends, and those I work with, in achieving their own personal goals. I also enjoy the contradictions that are part of everyone's behaviour and outlook, including my own.

One of my favorite Zen stories is of the man walking on the beach throwing starfish back into the water. When a friend asks him why, he says that putting them back in the water gives them a chance of life: otherwise they will dry up on the beach and die. The friend observes that there are thousands of starfish on the beach - so how can what he is doing make a difference? The man replies, as he throws yet another starfish back, 'Well, it has made a difference to this one!' I like to think that his friend then started to throw the starfish back too.

Dr Davida de la Harpe is a Consultant in Public Health Medicine, and has worked in the Irish health service for many years. She currently heads up the National Health Intelligence Unit in the Irish health service.

SELF-LOVE

The glory of God is the human person fully alive.
(Irenaeus, philosopher and theologian, second century)

THE BIBLE TELLS US, 'LOVE YOUR neighbour as yourself'. What it does not tell us is that we should love ourselves with our whole heart and mind and soul. So many people go through life with dreams in their heart, promising themselves that one day these will become reality, only to die full of regret and disappointment.

Many of the reasons we hold back are reasons in our minds only. They are not really barriers at all. To my mind, there is one purpose in life, and that is to live as fully as possible and be all that you can be. To do what you love doing as well as you can do it. You will be blessed with happiness and constantly creating yourself anew.

John O'Donohue reiterates the importance of self-realisation, in these lines from his book, *Anam Cara*: *'If you allow your nature to come alive, then everything will come into rhythm. If you live the life you love, you will receive shelter and blessings. Sometimes the great famine of blessing in and around us derives from the fact that we are not living the* life we love, rather, that we are living the life expected of us. We have fallen out of rhythm with the secret signature and light of our own nature.'

Liz O'Donnell describes the importance of respecting our own identities beautifully in her contribution, when she writes: *'For me, being in control of one's life is very important. Too many people allow family, friends and others to determine their destiny. One, of course, has responsibility to others, but fundamentally, autonomy and personal accountability is vital for self-worth and happiness.'*

As someone who is naturally cautious, I am envious of Grania Willis' spirit of adventure, and yet empathise with the need to step out of our comfort zones and take that first, most difficult step towards change. It takes courage to push the boundaries in order to realise one's full potential, and Grania sums this up beautifully in the line: *'the brave may not live forever, but the cautious do not live at all'*.

Self-love also requires, however, that we embrace our frailties, learn from our weaknesses and accept ourselves for what we are. In the words of Sr Stanislaus, in her book, *Stillness Through My Prayers*: *'I am strong when I embrace my weakness; I am a teacher when I can be taught; I enjoy others when I enjoy myself; I am wise when I accept my own foolishness; I find true laughter when I laugh at myself.'*

I think the secret lies in being patient, both with ourselves and with others.

GRANIA WILLIS

I'M NOT OFFICIALLY YOUNG ANY MORE, but I am, and always will be, young at heart. So I'm constantly looking for new challenges, and am never happier than when I've bitten off what many people would consider far too much of a mouthful.

My chief source of happiness is a challenge and the bigger it is, the happier I am. I can't wait to get out way out of my comfort zone and just go for it. *Carpe diem*, because if you don't seize the day, somebody else will steal it from under your nose!

But, all too often, getting started is the hardest part. Whatever the project, the first step is always the toughest, but it's sometimes hard to remember that every journey, no matter the distance, begins with that first step. Chinese philosopher Lao Tzu put it perfectly: '*The journey of a thousand miles begins with a single step.*' And it's true. When you've taken that first step, you just have to keep putting one foot in front of the other.

My challenges don't have to be physical ones, although undoubtedly those are the ones I prefer. I spent the latter part of 2007, and all of 2008, working in Hong Kong on the Olympic and Paralympic equestrian events and, although many of those 24/7 months were deskbound, it was physically and mentally draining. Just as tough as climbing a mountain and, in many ways, very similar.

A friend once said to me that climbing big mountains is a 'retrospective' sport, awful at the time, but amazing when you look back on it. Working on the Olympics was a bit like that. I had to constantly keep reminding myself of the words of climber and writer Dermot Somers, who once told me not to be so intent on my goal that I forgot to look at the view!

I've had some wonderful experiences. I've flown the flag for Ireland on the international equestrian circuit, I've planted the Tricolour on some of the world's highest mountains, and I've been privileged enough to be able to write about many of those experiences in the pages of *The Irish Times*. And now, I've worked backstage at an Olympics. But still I hanker for more.

The secret of youth is said to be doing something every day that scares you. That's getting out of your comfort zone in a big way, and reminds me of a quotation I came across recently. I don't know where it's from, but the sentiment is perfect and it has become my mantra: 'The brave may not live forever, but the cautious do not live at all.'

Remember that next time the comfort zone is beckoning!

Everest summiteer, Grania Willis' international riding career was brought to a premature end by life-threatening internal injuries and a broken back, but she has gone on to become a leading equestrian journalist, mountain climber, bestselling author, charity worker, motivational speaker and, briefly, a reality star on the RTÉ programme, Celebrity Jigs 'n' Reels. Despite her late start in the climbing world, Grania was the first Irish woman to climb the world's highest mountain via the northeast ridge, reaching the summit of Everest in June 2005.

Linda O'Shea Farren

THE CELTIC TIGER HAS STOPPED ROARING and we are 'in a different place', to put it mildly. Against all of the negatives of this change, we have been given the space we need to reflect on what it is we really want in our lives.

We should take this golden opportunity to get a grip on our lives, not on our possessions.

Ireland has come a long way, particularly in the past decade. And that is to be celebrated out loud. Nobody wants to go back to the bad old days, when famine ravaged our soil, when poverty drove us abroad, when inequality was the norm, when the 'haves' and the 'have-nots' were worlds apart, when Ireland was not at peace. We much prefer a time, '*when hope and history rhyme*', as Seamus Heaney would say.

But we seem to have mislaid (temporarily, at least) some of what makes this country and its people unique in the world. People have vehemently denied the 'Rip-Off Ireland' label, but we can all see plainly that there is truth in it. 'Ireland of the Thousand Welcomes' may seem like a corny tourism ploy, but unwelcoming people are as much a problem for those who live in a country as they are for tourists. Do we prefer chasing our tails constantly? Being stuck in traffic, morning, noon and night? Eating convenience foods on the run? I don't think so.

Have the simple pleasures of the past lost their appeal forever? How long is it since you took a flask and sandwiches to the beach? Climbed a mountain? Picked blackberries? Built a kid's trolley cart?

Diane Loomans's pearls of wisdom spring to mind:

> If I had my child to raise all over again
> I'd finger-paint more and
> point the finger less
> I would do less correcting and
> more connecting
> I'd take my eyes off my watch and
> watch with my eyes
> I would care to know less and
> know to care more
> I'd take more hikes and fly more kites
> I'd stop playing serious and seriously play
> I would run through more fields and
> gaze at more stars
> I'd do more hugging and less tugging
> I'd build self-esteem first and the house later
> I would be firm less often and
> affirm much more
> I'd teach less about the love of power

And much more about
the power of love ...

from *100 Ways to Build Self-esteem and Teach
Values* by Diana Loomans, 2005

We Irish are not only resilient and resourceful, we are also adaptive. We have a rich history. We have able young people. We have a bright future. We can, and will, build on the solid foundations this nation has laid.

But building our economy is only part of the picture. Every one of us has to build a life. And, together, our lives form the life of the nation.

Self-development is the path ahead. A selection of the many thought-provoking quotations of Eleanor Roosevelt might be a good place to start:

Friendship with oneself is all-important,
because without it, one cannot be
friends with anyone else in the world.

Great minds discuss ideas; average minds
discuss events; small minds discuss people.

People grow through experience if they
meet life honestly and courageously.
This is how character is built.

Learn from the mistakes of others.
You can't live long enough to make
them all yourself.

No one can make you feel inferior
without your consent.

Beautiful young people are accidents of
nature, but beautiful old people are
works of art.

Whatever can possibly happen any day can only pale by comparison to the loss of a loved one forever. You can only enjoy them while they are still with you, so why waste any time?

After many years as a New York lawyer, investment banker in Dublin, Programme Manager and Political Adviser at the Department of Justice and a Director at the Irish Wheelchair Association, Linda O'Shea Farren now has her own solicitor's practice, is an National University of Ireland Senator, Chairman of NUI Convocation and Non-Executive Director of the EBS. She is also a public advocate and regular media contributor in relation to issues as varied as politics, disability, education, music and shareholder rights.

GEOFFREY SPRATT

Music is the universal language of mankind
H. W. Longfellow

I'M A MUSICIAN, SO I HOPE you won't doubt me when I say, simply and objectively, ergo, I am a happy person and enjoy my life. However, I also hope that I will never fail to appreciate and value the fact that the core of my being is existing within a truly loving and stable family - wife, sons and daughters-in-law: thank you from the bottom of my heart.

I am privileged - and, yes, that is honestly and precisely the way I see it - to be the Director of the Cork School of Music. Although my job requires me to function as a manager rather than as a musician, I believe with passion as well as conviction that anything and everything I do needs to make it better, not worse, for everyone in the CSM - students and staff alike, as they strive to make progress on the lifelong learning path that becoming a musician involves. I am so fortunate: those with whom I work closest in the CSM are truly amazing colleagues. They all understand that real music-making cannot happen without the ultimate in teamwork and, as we all equate management and administration with music-making, they always inspire me to try to be a better 'team player' myself.

I also feel privileged to live in Cork. The city has so many cultural strands, and most of them need volunteers to enable them to flourish. I feel I can make a form of payback for my privileges by volunteering. The multiple and inexpressibly wonderful types of experiences I had as Director of the Cork International Choral Festival, Chairman of Cumann Náisiúnta na gCór and of the Music Association of Ireland, I am still able to have with the Cork Orchestral Society. The joys of having, in the past, conducted the UCC Choir and Orchestra, the UCC Choral Society, the Galway Baroque Singers and Madrigal '75, I still have with the Fleischmann Choir, Canticum Novum and the CSM Symphony Orchestra. They enrich my life and demand that I keep improving my musicianship. They are a source of great fulfilment, and fertile ground for friendships that are of infinite value. I don't have the time now to do much guest work with the RTÉ orchestras, but still learn so much from working regularly with the outstanding professionals in Dublin's Orchestra of St Cecilia.

In the words of H.D. Thoreau: '*Man is the artificer of his own happiness.*'

My personal indulgence is reading, and a weakness of mine is quoting from what I read when I speak in public or write something like this. As penance for my indulgence, I have contained myself this time. If the result is uninspiring, please accept my apologies. I am happy, and you can be too.

Geoffrey Spratt was a professional flautist and viola player, with a wide experience of choral, operatic and orchestral conducting with both amateur and professional ensembles, before coming to live and work in Ireland in 1976. Over the past thirty-three years, he has combined a career in music education while also having a significant input to various voluntary bodies working to further the cause of music in Ireland. Geoffrey lectured in the Music Department of UCC from 1976-92. In September 1992, he was appointed Director of the Cork School of Music.

EMMA DONOGHUE

On Work

THEN A PLOUGHMAN SAID:
'Speak to us of work.'
And he answered, saying:
'You work that you may keep pace with the earth and the soul of the earth.

For to be idle is to be a stranger unto the seasons, and to step out of life's procession, that marches in majesty and proud submission towards the infinite.

When you work you are a flute through whose heart the whispering of the hours turns to music.

Which of you would be a reed, dumb and silent, when all else sings together in unison?

Always you have been told that work is a curse, and labour a misfortune.

But I say to you that when you work you fulfil a part of earth's furthest dream, assigned to you when that dream was born,

And in keeping yourself with labour, you are in truth loving life,

And to love life with labour is to be intimate with life's inmost secret.

But if you in your pain call birth an affliction, and the support of the flesh a curse written on your brow, then I answer that naught but the sweat of your brow shall wash away that which is written.

You have been told also life is darkness, and in your weariness you echo what was said by the weary.

And I say that life is indeed darkness save when there is urge,

And all urge is blind save when there is knowledge,

And all knowledge is vain save when there is work,

And all work is empty save when there is love;

And when you work with love you bind yourself to yourself, and to one another, and to God.

And what is it to work with love?

It is to weave the cloth with threads drawn from your heart, even as your beloved were to wear that cloth.

It is to build a house with affection, even as if your beloved were to dwell in that house.

It is to sow seeds with tenderness and to reap the harvest with joy, even as if your beloved were to eat the fruit.

It is to charge all things you fashion with breath of your own spirit,

And to know that all the blessed dead are standing about you and watching.

Often have I heard you say, as if speaking in sleep, 'He who works in marble and finds the shape of his own soul in the stone, is nobler than he who ploughs the soil.

And he who seizes the rainbow to lay it on a cloth in

the likeness of man, is more than he who makes the sandals for our feet.'

But I say, not in sleep, but in the over-wakefulness of noon-tide, that the wind speaks not more sweetly to the giant oaks than to the least of all the blades of grass;

And he alone is great who turns the voice of the wind into a song made sweeter by his own loving.

Work is love made visible.

And if you cannot work with love but only with dis-taste, it is better that you should leave your work and sit at the gate of the temple and take alms of those who work with joy.

For if you bake bread with indifference, you bake a bitter bread that feeds but half man's hunger.

And if you grudge the crushing of the grapes, your grudge distils a poison in the wine.

And if you sing though as angels, and love not the singing, you muffle man's ears to the voices of the day and the voices of the night.'

from Kalil Gibran's *The Prophet*, 1923

Born in Dublin in 1969, Emma Donoghue now lives with her partner and their two children in Canada. She writes drama for stage and radio as well as literary history, but is best known for her fiction, in particular for her historical novels Slammerkin, Life Mask *and* The Sealed Letter.

LIZ O'DONNELL

FOR ME, BEING IN CONTROL OF one's life is very important. Too many people allow family, friends and others to determine their destiny. One, of course, has responsibility to others, but fundamentally autonomy and personal accountability is vital for self-worth and happiness.

I always had an independence of mind, and, indeed, was often disciplined at school for what was termed 'insubordination'. This independent streak made me challenging to parent and teachers at times, but it served me well in later life.

I was very privileged to study law at Trinity College, an experience that greatly influenced my outlook and values. Law at Trinity was taught as part of the Humanities rather than as a professional course, and I learned the importance of intellectual rigour and logic which informed my basic liberal philosophy.

The greatest influence, however, was my family. Integrity was perhaps the biggest gift my parents imparted to their children. My parents were not at all political but were active members of the community, with a strong instinct for public service and connectedness.

I never imagined that these values, absorbed unconsciously during my upbringing, would later inform a life of public service as a TD and government minister. Politics at that level is not for the faint-hearted. The instinct for intellectual independence, honed at Trinity by a liberal education, served me well, as did the confidence to make a decision and stand over it if I felt it was the right thing to do.

I tend to run with the ball if it is passed to me, and make the best of every opportunity. As for happiness, I think if you emit grace and optimism, it comes back to you in spades. People respond to positivity and a genuine smile. If one accepts that life was never meant to be a bed of roses, but is lined with challenges to test our mettle, each day becomes a wonderful gift.

Liz O'Donnell was a Progressive Democrat TD (Member of Parliament) for Dublin South for fifteen years. She was a Minister of State at the Department of Foreign Affairs from 1997 to 2002, and represented the Irish Government at the multi-party talks leading to the Good Friday Agreement. She also had responsibility for Ireland's Overseas Aid budget at a time of major expansion of the programme. Liz is a native of Dublin and an Honours Law graduate of Trinity College. She retired from politics in 2007, and now works in media and public affairs consultancy. She has two adult children.

Derval O'Rourke

To laugh often and much;
To win the respect of intelligent
people and the affection of children;
To earn the appreciation of honest
critics and endure the betrayal of
false friends;
To appreciate beauty, to find the
best in others;
To leave the world a bit better,
whether by a healthy child, a garden
patch or a redeemed social condition;
To even know one life has breathed
easier because you have lived:
This is to have succeeded.

Attributed to Ralph Waldo Emerson,
1803-1882

I often wonder about my determination and where it has come from. When I was growing up in Cork, I spent my whole life running around and playing. I was lucky, in that I had super parents who were strict when they needed to be but let me find my own feet.

I began running at seven and loved how it felt. I loved that feeling of running as fast as you can go, and the whole world stopping as you run. I used to do loads of races in GAA clubs on grass and I adored the thrill of it. There would always be a couple of girls that people would say were really fast and I loved the challenge of trying to be faster. I think that as I have got older, it has stayed the same, only the stakes have become higher.

I love running fast, mainly because I have always had a deep-rooted faith in my own ability. When I run to my potential, I think this faith is justified.

I am not sure from where or how this faith developed, but it is something that has consistently been there and grown over the years. I think I have been very influenced by certain people to have faith in myself. As a child, I had a few coaches and they all had a major impact. They taught me that you run faster if you work harder, that you must handle your defeats with grace, and that no matter how low you go, you must always bounce back.

I think that no matter what you do in life, people are the essence of it. For me, success would be meaningless without people to share it with. I'm happy to say that I have some amazing people in my life who inspire me all the time in their own ways. And I hope that I inspire them from time to time in my own little way.

Derval O'Rourke is an international athlete from Cork. She has won world and European medals in sprint hurdles. She has a BA in Sociology and Geography, and is currently studying for an MSc in Sociology of Sport and Exercise.

LARA MARLOWE

ONCE UPON A TIME THERE WAS A KING. The king asked the artists in his court to create a work of art that would make him happy when he was sad, and sad when he was happy. The royal jeweller made a ring, and on it was engraved: 'Everything passes in the end.'

How long time seems when one is young. How fleeting and precious it becomes with each passing year. How lucky are those painters and writers who manage, through their art, to reach out for and freeze passing moments.

By constantly making lists of things I must do, in the order they're to be done, I manage to impose order on chaos and meet my deadlines. If I start to feel overwhelmed, I repeat to myself a line from T.S. Eliot's 'The Love Song of J. Alfred Prufrock': '*There will be time, there will be time ...*' And somehow there always is.

When misfortune strikes, as it invariably does, I try to keep a sense of perspective. 'Nobody's injured. Nobody's dead,' I tell myself if I've lost money or property or suffered a set-back.

Happiness in the sense that we imagined it as children – as a state of permanent bliss – is unattainable. But satisfaction is a realistic goal. Though I long ago cast aside the more arcane aspects of existentialist philosophy, its basic tenets ring true for me: that, though existence is ultimately futile, we can create meaning in our lives. Saving the world was over-ambitious, a college professor told me years ago. If one could simply be careful not to hurt other people, one would have achieved a great deal.

Life is obviously easier for those of us who love what we do for a living. I often think that knowing what you really want to do is the hardest thing. When you are certain of what it is, it is only a matter of trying and trying, until you achieve it.

The highest moments are those rare occasions when you feel you've reached your potential: when, in my case, I've written the best possible article that could be written.

Fortunately, there are many simpler forms of contentment: the small kindnesses of friends and colleagues; a cat purring on one's knees; the endorphin high that comes from swimming; playing the piano. Riding a bicycle through Paris, especially on Sunday mornings when the streets are empty; the flying sensation that comes from cycling.

It's impossible to programme these moments of euphoria. They just happen, but it helps to be open to them. The memory of them sticks in your subconscious, so that when things get rough, you can find the fortitude within yourself to repeat like a mantra: 'Life is good.' The French call it *'la methode Coué'*. It's basically positive thinking, or self-persuasion. It's not a panacea, but it's a good start.

As a Paris-based foreign correspondent for The Irish Times *since 1996, Lara Marlowe covers French politics, culture and foreign policy. Her work has included writing on the aftermath of Israel's assault on the Gaza Strip (2009), the 'Inside Turkey' series for* The Irish Times *(2007), and the US bombardment and invasion of Iraq, with subsequent reporting trips describing the country's slide into chaos and civil war (2003-2005). Marlowe has also worked in Afghanistan and Algeria. She covered the breakup of Yugoslavia throughout the 1990s and the 1999 NATO bombardment of Serbia. Born in California, Lara holds degrees in French Literature and International Relations from UCLA, the Sorbonne and Oxford. In 2006, she was made a Chevalier de la Légion d'Honneur for her contribution to Franco-Irish relations.*

LISE HAND

THERE IS NOTHING MORE SCARIFYINGLY TERROR-INDUCING than a newspaper deadline. It is non-negotiable, unmoving and inexorable. It is impervious to the imprecations of a desperate journalist.

There are days when I sit there, Word document as blank as my brain, fingers poised over the keyboard. One hour to go before some irate editor starts issuing shouty threats down the phone line. One hour to abject failure and professional oblivion.

I get up and make a cup of tea. Rearrange the tottering pile of old newspapers on my desk, surf the net for oneway flights to Timbuktu, leaving imminently. Still nothing. Why did I choose journalism, instead of something easier and less stressful, like sword-swallowing or fire-eating? Why?

The trouble is, I'm not good at anything else except writing. (And today I'm not even good at that, it seems). I'm a lousy cook, useless at Maths and am barred from ever singing in public after that last debacle with a free microphone at a Fianna Fáil Ard Fheis.

Fifty minutes to go now. Squeaky bum time. I offer up a prayer to my god of the day – the deity varies, depending on what inspiration is required. It could be Raymond Chandler, James Joyce, Pablo Neruda, Hunter S. Thompson, Truman Capote or – in times of serious trouble – St Dorothy Parker.

Is this room getting hotter, or is it just me? The first beads of sweat drip onto the keyboard. My mind is devoid of wit. I'm a halfwit. I've just spent an hour in the Dáil, listening to the Taoiseach drone on about paradigms and parameters. Surely any fool can effortlessly craft 800 words of polished, entertaining prose about that? Anyone, except me.

And then, rising like a salmon out of the river of self-pity, comes a sentence, sleek and fully formed. I greedily grasp it in mid-leap and hurl it down on the page. Thank Jaysus, that'll do for an intro.

The joyful sound of tapping fills the room. All the other sounds fade away. That stillness of concentration wraps around me like a blanket. Words come creeping out of their hidingplaces and offer themselves up for my consideration. The jigsaw takes shape – a bit of observation, a couple of pertinent quotes, a pun or two.

Two minutes to go. Save. Copy. Paste. Send.

Sigh. Not too bad, considering. If I'd had more time, of course, it would've been a masterpiece, held up in journalism courses all over the world as a shining example of our trade. But still, there's always tomorrow.

Time for a pint. God, I love my job. It terrifies me, stresses me and occasionally reduces me to whimpers. But it's what I do best, writing, and I never seem to tire of the sheer exhilaration of the daily wrestle to do better.

It'll never make me rich. But with every deadline defeated, it'll forever make me happy.

Lise Hand is a political sketchwriter for the Irish Independent. *She has also worked for the* Sunday Independent, *the* Sunday Tribune, *countless magazines and even (for a short, glorious spell) the* New York Daily News *and the* New York Post. *Lise has served time as a news reporter, features writer, arts editor, social diarist and magazine editor in order to make a crust. In between, she was a damn fine waitress.*

NIALL O'HIGGINS

Cancer – *Tenebrae Cedant Luci*

HE WAS AN INSPIRING MAN. As Chief Psychiatrist in St Joseph's Psychiatric Hospital in Limerick, my father introduced several improvements in care. He was particularly active in attempting to overcome the damaging social stigma associated with mental illness. He designed the hospital badge, showing a nursing hand drawing a dark curtain back from the bedside with the motto: '*Tenebrae Cedant Luci*' ('Let darkness yield to light').

The stigma associated with cancer has parallels with that of psychiatric illness. The mistaken belief that the diagnosis of cancer is a signal of impending death often led to a fatalistic attitude, resulting in diagnostic delay and suboptimal care.

Diagnosis of cancer can also lead to social isolation. I have frequently experienced bedside interchanges among relatives, using exaggerated movements of the lips to mouth the word 'cancer'. No spoken words or even whispers were exchanged, lest the patient in the bed hear the fatal word.

Four related factors stimulated my special interest in cancer care: the stigma and lack of knowledge about cancer; the huge inequalities in access to good care between countries and regions; the evidence that results are best when cancer specialists work together; the value of involvement in research activity. This interest in cancer soon became a professional preoccupation, an obsession, even.

Although cancer remains an elusive enemy, an enormous body of knowledge now exists about its biological mechanisms, its prevention and its treatment. Cancers previously considered fatal are now curable. Common cancers, if identified in the early stages, can be cured by expert and effective treatment. Yet there remains a gap, some would say a chasm, between public knowledge about cancer and the tremendous advances in care and cure.

In 2005, 11 million new cases of cancer were diagnosed globally, and there were 7 million deaths due to cancer. In the year 2030, 27 million cancers will be diagnosed globally, while 17 million deaths from cancer will occur. The increased incidence of the illness will be due to: (i) the global population increase, from 6.45 billion in 2005 to over 8 billion in 2030; (ii) longer life-span: two-thirds of those over 65 years of age who ever lived are alive today, and (iii) the introduction of the risk factors for cancer from developed countries to poorly resourced countries will be added to those already existing there. Approximately 43 per cent of cancer deaths could be prevented, because they are due to tobacco, diet and infections. This alarming figure represents a huge challenge in cancer prevention efforts worldwide.

Improved cure rates are, however, being reported from all around the globe. 25 million people are alive today following cancer treatment, and this number will rise to 75 million by the year 2030 - a remarkable demonstration of improving care.

Many cancers are now curable because of:

♦ Better diagnosis, which combines increasing accuracy with the minimising of error. Cancers are now identifiable when they are at an early stage in their development. Abnormalities can even be discovered before they become cancerous. Population-based screening reduces death rates from the common fatal cancers.

♦ Advances in treatment, due largely to clinical trials comparing newer treatments with older therapies, and laboratory-based cancer research. Understanding the basic biological characteristics of individual cancers has led to the development of treatments that are specifically targeted at the cancer cells.

♦ Improved accountability in measuring quality of care. Clinical auditing raises standards. Evidence across the globe indicates the value of specialist cancer centres in improving survival and quality of life. Comparisons with international norms provide reassurance and information to patients, relatives, doctors, communities and policy-makers.

♦ Training of cancer specialists – surgical oncologists, medical oncologists, radiation oncologists, radiologists, pathologists, palliative care specialists, specialist nurses, psychologists and many others – has improved results. Multi-professional and multidisciplinary team meetings among experts have been of considerable benefit to people with cancer.

♦ Enormous collaboration exists among researchers, clinicians and educational institutions worldwide, producing spectacular progress towards excellence and helping eliminate the inequalities in cancer care between nations and regions of the world.

'*Tenebrae Cedant Luci.*'

Niall O'Higgins was Professor of Surgery at UCD in St Vincent's Hospital from 1977 until his retirement in 2007. He has been involved – in Ireland and throughout the world – in promoting improvements in cancer care and the training of cancer specialists, especially in breast cancer. He was founding President of the Irish Society of Surgical Oncology and was President of the European Society of Surgical Oncology, the World Federation of Surgical Oncology Societies and the Federation of European Cancer Societies. He was President of the Royal College of Surgeons in Ireland from 2004 –2006. At present he is Professor and Chairman of the Department of Surgery in the Royal College of Surgeons in Ireland-Medical University of Bahrain.

MICHAEL FLATLEY

NOTHING IS IMPOSSIBLE.

Michael Flatley is an Irish-American step dancer, writer, flautist, choreographer and occasional television presenter who became internationally known through his theatre musicals, Lord of the Dance and others. Michael first shot to fame during the interval of the 1994 Eurovision Song Contest.

☙

Mary Kelly Quinn

Opportunity

John J. Ingalls, 1891

Master of human destinies am I,
Fame, love and fortune
on my footsteps wait.
Cities and field I walk. I penetrate
Deserts and seas remote, and, passing by
Hovel and mart and palace, soon or late,
I knock unbidden once at every gate.

The brief I was given for my contribution to this collection
of writing was very broad yet challenging for someone like
me, who had not previously taken the time to articulate a
'philosophy', 'motivation' or 'approach' for living life.

After some thought, and looking back at my student days and
a career in education and research spanning some twenty
years, I feel our attitude and response to opportunity have the
greatest potential to shape our lives and provide real challenge
and joy. My life has been blessed with so many opportunities

provided by people who better understood their significance, yet left the choice entirely to me.

Participation in the Young Scientist of the Year competition was probably the most significant opportunity in my life, an opportunity that came in the guise of a simple question from a dedicated teacher, 'Would you like to do a project?' My 'yes' brought a significant workload from a hard taskmaster, but also unfolded so many other opportunities that far outweighed the effort required. Indeed, what young people sometimes fail to understand is that the fruits of opportunity are not always immediately obvious, are generally not defined and are certainly not gained without some element of hard work and openness to the guidance of those who point them in the right direction. As the American inventor and businessman, Thomas A. Edison, apparently wrote: '*Opportunity is missed by most people because it is dressed in overalls and looks like work.*'

Fortunately, today, most young people in Ireland have the opportunity to avail of third-level education, something most of their parents could not even have dreamed of. It is a unique chance to capitalise on one's talents and interests, and aim for a career that brings fulfilment. But here again, if this opportunity is to yield its full potential, it needs to be grasped with the enthusiasm and application that it deserves.

We can spend a lifetime waiting for opportunity to happen, or recognise it in all life's chances, no matter how insignificant. I recently received a thank-you card from Mike in Ghana, a student who had spent a summer working with my research group in University College Dublin. What he wrote sums up beautifully an appreciation of the chances life may offer: '*Thank you for one of the greatest gifts in life – opportunity.*'

Mary Kelly Quinn is a lecturer in the School of Biology and Environmental Science at UCD. As a freshwater biologist, her main research interest is in the assessment of human impacts and land use activities on water quality and the ecological health of Irish rivers and lakes. Mary is a former winner of the Young Scientist Exhibition and is still involved with the competition as a judge.

FREEDOM OF MIND

FREEDOM OF MIND, TO ME, IS an ability to take charge of your emotions and keep control at times of provocation. Ann Henning Jocelyn describes this beautifully in her book, *Keylines for Living*, when she says: *'The more strongly a feeling manifests itself, the more superficial it is. Using moods to let off steam, indulge ourselves, or even manipulate others, is a means to an end not altogether honourable. Emotional responses need not affect our conduct. Like spoilt children, they crave attention, but once we recognise them, they settle down.'*

Very often, an emotional response is a learned reaction to a particular stimulus. In the same way, we can identify the response as a learned reaction and choose to react in a different way, thus exercising control over our immediate impulses. I find this very useful when dealing with young children who are experts at demanding a reaction. By choosing not to react, not only do I choose a path that proffers a solution, but I also teach my children to react with a cool head. This is easier said than done. But being aware is the first step.

Yet emotions also have their place in helping us to create freedom: the freedom to be ourselves. This is highlighted in Patricia Redlich's gentle, commonsense piece about the importance of passion in our lives. Everyone has something they love doing. It is up to us to encourage them to find their talents and the source of their passion, and support them all the way, so that they have the space and freedom to achieve their full potential.

Once again, practising silence can often be the first step to achieving true freedom of mind. As Neale Donald Walsch observes in his book, *Conversations with God*, although initially we may find ourselves overwhelmed with superficial chatter and noise, if we are able to persist in silence: '*... the silence deepens, and we begin to connect with our real nature and understand the distinction between who we really are and the person we have constructed for our self. You will learn not to be the fittest, strongest, cleverest, but to be the most loving: then you will experience the full glory of Who you really are.*'

Mark Patrick Hederman

AT A VERY EARLY AGE - AROUND about nine years old, if I remember rightly - I had to make a big decision: either I was God, or there was another. I had to admit, after some calculation, that the first scenario was improbable. The second required some effort from me to get in contact with whoever was in charge of this universe, into which I had been thrown without my permission. I have never doubted that there was such a person, or, as it turns out, persons (*pace* Dawkins *et al*). Maintaining that contact and putting myself at the disposal of these distant, reticent, ingeniously nimble-fingered and intimate persons, who constantly guide us towards the goal for which we were intended since the beginning of time - despite their ludicrous insistence upon our free will to screw up every attempt of theirs to bring this to fruition - has been for me the most fulfilling life I could have imagined, even if the first option had been a possibility!

Mark Patrick Hederman has been a monk of Glenstal Abbey for over forty years. Formerly headmaster of the school there, he has lectured in philosophy and literature in America and Nigeria, as well as in Ireland. He is also the author of several books, including Kissing the Dark: Connecting with the Unconscious, The Haunted Inkwell: Art and our Future *and* Walkabout: Life as Holy Spirit.

was n... ...y was, he had nothing. Maybe he had hum-
... ...rn... and ... his profit, his life, the ... day down

◆

Sebastian Barry

Angel

I was hurrying up the escalator of the Angel tube station in
London, on my way to rehearsals in Islington and late as usual.
There was a great stream of people going up, going down. In
the ticket area at the top were a hundred and more people, all
intently heading from the stairs to the sunlit doorways.

Coming across at an angle to all these people, like a salmon
fly dragged against the current, was a man on his own. He
was small, thin, grey, about my own age, with a long, still
face. He seemed too old to be a drug addict, somehow. The
curious thing was, he passed through the people as if he had
no bodily substance at all, and certainly no one looked at
him. He didn't bump into anyone, but seemed to know how
to move through a crowd of souls without hindrance. He was
obviously real, but at the same time seemed to exist at an
angle to everyone else, just as his passage across the room was
at an angle to everyone else.

I looked at him with great curiosity as I passed him. He didn't
meet my eye, didn't expect anyone to see him, maybe. What

248

was most likely was, he had nothing. Maybe he had had family, fortune and children, but now he looked absolutely alone. His clothes were covered in a slight dust, like someone who had walked through an explosion. It struck me that this man, men like him, people like him, were often written about in Irish literature, most famously in Yeats and Beckett: the wandering tramp, the homeless person. And I wondered, as I passed, if this man might not know a secret that everyone should ask him about, and that would benefit anyone that asked? Seemingly mired in poverty, he appeared to be the most human creature there - alone, poised, indifferent, possibly even hopeful of the day: how could I know? And permanently, persistently, perfectly, moving against the tide.

Sebastian Barry was born in Dublin between the canals in 1955. He went to the Catholic University School and then to Trinity College Dublin. His plays include The Steward of Christendom, *and* The Pride of Parnell Street, *and his novels,* A Long, Long Way, *and* The Secret Scripture. *Sebastian lives in Wicklow with his wife and their three children.*

PATRICIA REDLICH

I ONLY RECENTLY REALISED THAT, SOMETIME very early in life, I learned the happy knack of enjoying whatever task I had to do, rather than resenting it. That doesn't involve being a sucker who is constantly dumped on. It just means that if you have to study, or cut the grass, or mind the baby brother, then you do it willingly. It's to do with seeing the necessities of life as challenges, rather than impositions.

Charm is a skill to be seriously cherished. It eases awkward social moments. It makes other people feel good. It enables you to assert yourself without offending. It's about good humour, respect, warmth and politeness. A charming person is tactful, yet truthful. It makes it possible to be entirely real without being insensitive. And, of course, charm comes with a smile.

Passion, or enthusiasm, doesn't just make us attractive to others - it feeds our spirit. It's an essential element of being truly alive. Until we've found something to be passionate about, we're simply skimming the surface of existence.

Finally, one comment about myself. I don't ever give up.

I just change direction when I reach a dead end. Sometimes, that involves a compromise. Sometimes it involves recognising that there is such a thing as an unmanageable situation. It may be that I have to accept that I can't have exactly what I'm striving for. I may even have to learn to like something that seemed initially unattractive. But it's never about giving up, or despairing, or being defeated. It's always about that exciting process of conquering obstacles.

Patricia Redlich grew up in Dublin. After going to university in Germany, she practised as a clinical psychologist with the health service in Ireland. She has been an Agony Aunt with the Sunday Independent for the past twenty-five years.

MICHAEL VINEY

A CHANGED VIEW OF TIME IS one of the really momentous recognitions of the other, self-directed life. From waiting for Friday, for Christmas, for the holidays, you are suddenly free to live in the present: what shall I do today? But, sneaking in with that excitement, comes another revelation. It alighted on me suddenly when, one day, I was pushing the bicycle up the bog road.

I was fifty or so. For most of my life, I had been postponing happiness to some other time and place. Part of the frustration was all the time a journalist wastes, just hanging around for other people, or for the world to turn. Now, by some rashness and sleight of hand, I had wangled my way into the future: this was it. I had better be happy today, or else. If I was not, there was no one left to blame.

from *A Year's Turning* by Michael Viney, 1997

Writer and naturalist, Michael Viney's weekly column on ecology and rural living, 'Another Life', has appeared in The Irish Times *since 1977. His most recent book, written with his wife, Ethna, is* Ireland's Ocean: a Natural History.

MICHELLE SMITH DE BRUIN

MY PHILOSOPHY ON LIFE IS BASED on positive outlook and perseverance.

Thomas Foxwell Buxton said, '*With ordinary talent and extraordinary perseverance, all things are attainable*'. However, our greatest glory is, in the words of the American essayist and poet, Ralph Waldo Emerson, '*not in never falling, but in rising up every time we fall*'.

'*The race is not always to the swift, but to those who keep on running*.' The author of this saying is unknown, but it is believed to be a reference to the biblical passage in Ecclesiastes 9:11: '*I returned and saw under the sun, that the race is not to the swift, nor the battle to the strong, neither yet bread to the wise, nor yet riches to men of understanding, nor yet favour to men of skill, but time and chance happeneth to them all.*'

Michelle Smith de Bruin BL won three gold medals and one bronze medal for swimming at the 1996 Olympic Games in Atlanta. She won seven medals at European Championships during her swimming career and was also the holder of a European record. Michelle is currently practising as a barrister.

of international schools for peace studies. Students analyse

PAULINE BEWICK

THE MAIN MOTIVATION, ALBEIT UNCONSCIOUS, IN my painting is to understand the natural world, the people in it and myself. There isn't enough space in my brain to suss it all out mentally. I am identifying, through painting, the questions life and the world throws up, often through painting an idyllic moment.

As a teenager, I made up a calypso which went as follows: 'Overpopulation, overpopulation, overpopulation – that's the trouble with the whole world ...'

Overpopulation creates environmental problems – pollution, energy, housing, roads, schooling. My personal beliefs are: contraception should be openly talked about; wanted children will be loved; single parents should be considered totally natural and normal; extended families – i.e. relatives and the village or neighbours – will all feel a connection with other people's children. This would lessen the pain of parental separation. Affairs would be considered part of life, and accepted.

Overpopulation also causes aggression – as people fight for space and dominance. Around the world, we have a number of international schools for peace studies. Students analyse how and why war happens. One answer is to provide an outlet for aggressions – i.e. battlefields to fight it out on, leaving the rest of society not involved in it.

Overpopulation is now being broadly discussed by such people as Al Gore in his work, *An Inconvenient Truth*, Iain Stewart in his television series, *Earth: The Power of the Planet*, and David Attenborough in his film, *The State of our Planet*.

Another obsession I have always had was a wish for world government. World government would distribute food worldwide without barter, and with trust, in the knowledge that each human being has a talent and will give of themselves – even an hour a day – to society. '*Doing your best with what you are best at*', as Charles Handy said.

A country's leader should be chosen primarily for their calm, good-natured attitude to life – such as Barack Obama, who, it seems, has this attitude. These leaders would be put together for world government, to calmly work things out.

As far as health and foods go, people should be educated regarding healthy food, and the government should be responsible for banning additives and genetic modification and for organising environmentally wise farming. The same goes for fishing and the humane killing of animals.

Ideally, vegetarianism makes for more fields growing green

for our environment, and fewer animals polluting with methane gas. Vegetarianism has also been proven to make humans less aggressive.

Addressing the subject of aggression, bullies, murderers, paedophiles, and so on, should be dealt with in an incapacitating manner, rather than them being imprisoned. In the case of paedophiles, castration should be considered. To release testosterone, provision for sport, art and theatre should be of prime importance. Where the person is completely anti-social (e.g. a psychopath), a civilised, comfortable prison would be necessary.

Philosophies taught in schools should include Christianity, Islam, Buddhism, Taoism, Atheism (as in Richard Dawkins' series of lectures, 'Growing up in the Universe'), rather than just one religion.

Truth should be practised in all fields – with children first and foremost, and on into adulthood, their jobs, marriage, business, government, etc.

The truth about sexuality, homosexuality, lesbianism and promiscuity should not be hidden, nor should we pretend they don't exist.

The homeless, tramps, prostitutes and drug addicts should be accepted in society as needing help, in the form of shelters, public baths and free soup. Drug addicts should be brought through their addiction to be cured or to die. It is their choice. In terms of prostitution, health should be paramount, in order to prevent the spread of disease.

Euthanasia should be accepted for the terminally ill, after in-depth counselling. Suicide should not be considered wrong.

Dr Kefarelli, a man I met in Western Samoa, would stand on the great, black lava boulders that made up a small harbour and gaze out to the setting sun over the lagoon. 'I came here to the South Pacific to lead a more natural life. I married a woman with big, natural feet, her toes wide apart, and when I took her to my country, Italy, she cried because her feet were too big for the tiny, pointed, high-heeled shoes high society was wearing in Italy. I loved her for her closeness to nature, the way she would fish and grate coconuts for milk. She, it turns out, loved me for my four-wheel drive, the fridge we could afford and the only house with walls. I admired the women giving birth with the aid of the village around them. When I first came, it was a question of the survival of the fittest, and how I do Caesarean sections. Am I creating weaker human beings who will eventually be unable to give birth naturally?'

Poor Dr Kefarelli, his thin body with a piece of cloth tied around his hips, was a tortured soul. I think all philosophers are tortured. I would love to come across a laughing philosopher, one who believed in dancing and singing with joy at the funerals of life.

So, since I was very young, I have painted my personal life's questions. An argument with my mother, the latest crush, to have or not have babies, the change of life, old age and now having reached my seventies, I am looking outside myself, and am painting the strength and magnificence of nature without my personal emotions.

Pauline Bewick was born in 1935 in Northumbria, England, and moved to Ireland in 1937. The formative influence in her early life was her mother, 'Harry', and, at two-and-a-half years old, Pauline did her first pencil sketch, progressing within a few years to oils. In 1950, Pauline went to Dublin Art School, where she met Pat Melia, whom she eventually married and settled with in Kerry. She later had two daughters, Poppy and Holly. The past thirty years have seen Pauline's work develop an internationally recognisable style and become an integral part of Ireland's cultural legacy. She continues to follow her own path, and over the years she has created characters and themes that help reflect her own philosophies. On turning seventy in 2005, Pauline donated her master collection of paintings to the state. Two vast collections, representing the seven decades of her life to date, are permanently exhibited in Waterford and Killorglin.

JOSEPH O'CONNOR

MY GRANDMOTHER USED TO HAVE A prayer book she kept in her handbag. She'd tear poems and bits of newspaper articles and recipes out of the newspaper, and keep them between its flimsy pages. There were old photographs, too, and memorial cards, and letters, and loved ones' addresses in England and Canada: mementoes of various kinds, things she liked to keep close to her. The book amassed itself like a cairn, a scrapbook, a treasury. As a child, I loved looking through its contents: I felt I was being admitted to her heart. Over time, the book grew plumper, so that, by the last years of her life she could only close it by wrapping a thick elastic band around it.

I think we all acquire a sort of emotional prayer book as we go through life, a compendium of the small things we value. For some of us, as for my grandmother, it includes actual prayers; for others, it might contain memories and daydreams and jokes, or Bob Dylan songs, or stories, or bits from novels and poems. A first kiss. A beloved face. An insight someone once gave us.

So, here's one of the pages in my secret prayer book. It's pinned up over my desk and every time I have to do anything hard, I read it. It's a wonderful paragraph that was written by one of the greats, and I find it moving, sustaining, inspiring, calming, and resonant with a quiet joy and truthfulness. It makes me know I can face the difficult and that all will be well. I love it the way my grandmother used to love the mysteries of the rosary, and every time I read it, I remember her.

If he and his father and grandfather had torn the porch down themselves, he would have remembered so heroic a labour, as he did the smashing of the lath-and-plaster partition that separated the two small parlours downstairs, making one big living room, or the tearing out of the big stone kitchen fireplace and its chimney, right up into the attic. He remembered swinging the great stones out the attic window, he and his grandfather pushing, trying not to pinch their fingers, while his father, his face white with the effort, held the rope of a makeshift pulley rigged over a rafter. Once clear of the sill, the heavy stones fell with a strange slowness, seen from above, and accumulated into a kind of mountain it became Joey's summer job to clear away. He learned a valuable lesson that first summer on the farm, while he turned fourteen: even if you manage to wrestle only one stone into the wheelbarrow and sweatily, staggeringly, trundle it down to the swampy area this side of the springhouse, eventually the entire mountain will be taken away.

from 'A Sandstone Farmhouse', from *The Afterlife: and other stories* by John Updike, 1994

Joseph O Connor is the author of six novels: Cowboys and Indians, Desperadoes, The Salesman, Inishowen, Star of the Sea *and* Redemption Falls. *He has also written stage plays, film scripts and journalistic pieces, and contributes a popular weekly diary to RTÉ Radio 1's* Drivetime *programme.*

Fr Gearóid Dullea

THE FIRST PIECE IS TAKEN FROM the last chapter of St John's gospel, John 21:15-18. This scene captures so much that is significant in our relationship with God, the struggle to discern God's will for us and our attempts to make sense of this. Misunderstanding by Peter; constant patience on the part of the Lord; the tension around being asked to go somewhere one would rather not go; the centrality of love (even though the original language of the text here has an interesting play on different words for love); the command to care for others, and so forth. These are just some of the salient features that come to life when I read this passage.

When they had finished breakfast, Jesus said to Simon Peter: 'Simon, son of John, do you love me more than these?' He said to him: 'Yes, Lord: you know that I love you.' He said to him: 'Feed my lambs.'

A second time, He said to him: 'Simon, son of John, do you love me?' He said to him: 'Yes, Lord: you know that I love you.' He said to him: 'Tend my sheep.'

He said to him the third time: 'Simon, son of John, do

you love me?' Peter was grieved, because he said to
him the third time: 'Do you love me?' And he said to
him: 'Lord, you know everything, you know that I
love you.'

Jesus said to him: 'Feed my sheep. Truly, truly, I say to
you, when you were young, you girded yourself and
walked where you would; but when you are old, you
will stretch out your hands, and another will gird you
and carry you where you do not wish to go.' (This he
said to show by what death he was to glorify God.)
And after this he said to him: 'Follow me.'

The second piece is from the gospel of St Luke, a scene that
is prayed through every day in the Angelus prayer, the
Annunciation: Luke 1:26-38. The scene has had a profound
place in Western art, being the subject of fabulous represen-
tations down through the centuries. Moreover, it traces the
call and response of the whole Christian vocation.

In this dialogue between the Angel Gabriel and Mary, I find
a marvellous insight into the great human search for peace,
freedom and integrity. These great gifts are found ultimately
in the peace, freedom and integrity that God offers us and
asks of us. The delicate interplay between human freedom
and God's invitation – here between Mary's fear and hesita-
tion, and God's request that she become the mother of His
Son – is shown with sensitivity and inspiration. The endur-
ing wisdom of this passage is, I think, twofold: first, that our
seemingly small decisions can have enormous consequences,

in this case even leading to the full revelation of God; and second, that our deepest happiness is found in being who and where God wants us to be.

In the sixth month, the angel Gabriel was sent from God to a city of Galilee named Nazareth, to a virgin betrothed to a man whose name was Joseph, of the house of David; and the virgin's name was Mary. And he came to her and said: 'Hail, oh favoured one, the Lord is with you!' But she was greatly troubled at the saying, and considered in her mind what sort of greeting this might be. And the angel said to her: 'Do not be afraid, Mary, for you have found favour with God. And behold, you will conceive a son, and you shall call his name Jesus. He will be great and will be called the Son of the Most High; and the Lord God will give to Him the throne of his father David, and he will reign over the house of Jacob for ever; and of his kingdom, there will be no end.'

And Mary said to the angel: 'How shall this be, since I have no husband?' And the angel said to her: 'The Holy Spirit will come upon you, and the power of the Most High will overshadow you, therefore the child to be born will be called holy, the Son of God. And behold, your kinswoman Elizabeth in her old age has also conceived a son, and this is the sixth month with her who was called barren. For with God, nothing will be impossible.' And Mary said: 'Behold, I am the handmaiden of the Lord; let it be done to me according to your word.' And the angel departed from her.

Gearóid Dullea is a native of Bandon, Co. Cork, and a priest of the Diocese of Cork and Ross. Following postgraduate studies in theology, he served as chaplain in Cork University Hospital, and currently works as Co-ordinator of the Formation Programme for the Permanent Diaconate of the Irish Episcopal Conference.

Mary Kenny

The Best Thing I Ever Did

IN THE ANNALS OF MY LIFE, it was one of the best things I ever did. And, as time goes by, I am ever more grateful for having achieved it.

The best thing I ever did was to quit drinking alcohol. Maybe the worst thing I ever did – and there would be some competition for that particular award – was to start in the first place, but when you are seventeen and you are offered a glass of champagne, why wouldn't you accept it?

Anyway, I am not a puritan about drink. Alcohol, taken in a normal manner, can add pleasure, conviviality, merriment and *joie de vivre* to life, and I am all in favour of these things.

Nor am I in sympathy with those lists of regret categorised as: 'Things I wish I had known at twenty'. The truth about life is that it is an experiment in trial and error. And you only find out your errors by committing them.

With liquor, though, the pity is that in carrying out this experiment, you can inflict so much damage on other people. And give such bad example to the young and impressionable. That is the pain of regret that haunts old boozers.

Because, for those with addiction problems, alcohol is lethal. For the alcohol addict, he – or she – might as well be drinking arsenic. Slowly but ineluctably, an alcoholic is destroyed by alcohol. Just as the alcoholic slowly but ineluctably destroys all around him or her.

Many of the campaigns against alcohol focus on the damage that liquor can do – and truthfully so. But seldom is the pleasure of sobriety underlined: the appreciation of life in all its clarity; the delights of memory undisturbed by a haze of drunken forgetfulness; the way in which the whole narrative of existence is infused with enhanced animation. And less clouded by shame – not to speak of throbbing headaches and suicidally depressing hangovers.

Sobriety is the radiance of life, I would even say. Drunkenness is the avoidance of full experience.

I now see that I drank excessively and problematically for a number of reasons, including fear. Underneath a surface of boldness, there was a great deal that I feared, and couldn't face. As a young reporter, I was terrified half the time, and could only still those fears with large helpings of gin and tonic (and easy on the tonic).

'I drank to drown my sorrows, but my sorrows learned to swim.' Corny, but true.

Then, when faced with the suggestion that I should stop drinking, I was catatonic with melancholy at the thought of quitting. Without a drink, I'd be so lonely! I'd have no friends! Nothing to comfort me! Nothing to help me celebrate! Never again a jolly lunch with those reckless words, which Kingsley Amis once said were the most cheering in the English language, '*Shall we have the third bottle?*'

And I think that is the hardest thing for the drinker to contemplate: renouncing the comfort and conviviality of booze. Not to mention the taste of fine wines and fizzing champagne.

I'd never have been able to get sober without support, and above all, without this philosophy: a day at a time. You don't quit drinking forever. You just don't drink today.

And thus does one today lead to another, and gradually, a new world of savouring life – rather than seeking oblivion from it – reveals itself in all its glorious technicolour.

It's difficult to express the raptures of sobriety without sounding like a Salvation Army preacher. Yet sobriety's pleasures aren't advertised half enough.

Quitting alcohol is not a gloomy or a killjoy decision. It is about embracing life to the full, and feeling at top pitch the intoxication of heighted awareness. It is the ultimate act of freedom from a chemical which, for perhaps 15 per cent of the population, is simply lethal.

Mary Kenny has been a writer and journalist for four decades. Her most recent book is Crown and Shamrock: Love and Hate between Ireland and the British Monarchy.

Maurice Neligan

I DIDN'T HAVE A LIFE PLAN. It unfolded around me, part serendipity, part interest and, undoubtedly, part ambition. I didn't come from a medical family, and I think it was reading that persuaded me that maybe I had that mysterious thing much in vogue in our time: a vocation. I certainly wanted to become a doctor and, once involved, I took to it like the proverbial duck. It was an all-encompassing life, acquiring the knowledge and experience necessary to make you a functioning member of an honourable profession. I had no doubt then and have none now that what we are about is not self-centred. It was the call of helping your fellows in their time of need. It was basically about trying to extend the time between the cradle and the grave, and making it as comfortable as possible.

Early in your career, you realised that there were major limitations to what you could achieve, but you pushed away at remoulding the therapeutic landscape around you, and with your brethren around the world, altered the perspective and prognosis of illness. The realisation that the boundaries always remained, no matter how hard you tried and how much ground you made, was humbling. There was a much bigger plan out there and we could only do our best, our very best according to the standard of the time.

It was not that I thought about such things every day – I don't suppose anybody did, but it was always there in the background, driven by that other mysterious concept from my schooldays: conscience.

Conscience was always there, to assess your actions and ensure you gave your best and didn't quit. It wouldn't go away. Its fellow, compassion, was never far away and, sometimes, it was all you could offer.

You grew to accept the limits of your striving. Harder to accept was the failure of those supposedly in power to provide the basic facilities to enable those such as I to pursue our calling to look after the sick, irrespective of income or prestige. In retirement, I am motivated by the desire to see a caring and comprehensive service develop for all our people. There is a long way to go.

Maurice Neligan is a former Director of the National Cardiac Surgical Unit and Consultant Cardiac Surgeon, Mater Hospital and Our Lady's Hospital for Sick Children, Crumlin. He trained both in the UK and in the USA, at Blackrock College and at UCD. Maurice is now a columnist with The Irish Times. *Pastimes include golf, reading and nature. He is married to Pat, who is also a doctor and they had seven children.*

Sr Bernadine Meskell

Did you ever receive an unexpected letter that coaxed a response? Well, I received two such letters recently, in response to a radio interview I did with Ryan Tubridy on his morning show.

The first one asked me to write a paragraph or two for a book – which is what I am doing now!

The second letter asked me, among other things, how I thought St Clare of Assisi, our foundress, would have expressed her contemplative experience.

I think that to express this experience, Clare used the metaphor of a mirror, well known in the Middle Ages, but which she made original, by applying it to Jesus Christ as much in His divinity as in His humanity. The great teachers of contemplation speak of steps, stages, measures or degrees. Clare's is a simple method which germinates from experience, and is not entangled in lengthy explanations and considerations. It can be summed up in three verbs that appear in letters to her sister, St Agnes of Assisi: look, consider, contemplate.

For Clare, the Son of God became the Way, by assuming our humanity in the form of a servant. At the same time He became a mirror. Ours is a 'mirror-way' where we see reflected the poverty, the humility and the love of the Son of God: the Crib, the Cross and the Eucharist. To contemplate this mirror every day, continually, is to know the contemplative experience of Clare of Assisi.

On the same day these letters reached me, I also received in the post a book from a friend in Australia, and among the lovely verses was this poem that sums up nicely some of the fruits of contemplation:

To Be On Fire
from *The Wilds of the Heart*
by Noel Davis, 2003

Be still and know ...
not from hearsay
from experience

the wisdom
borne on the gentle breeze

the way that opens
in the quiet of patience

the Light
that dispels all our fears

our heart's desire
to be on Fire

the bigger reality, its clarity
seen from our contemplative place

the turning round of our world
that comes of being still

the freedom that flows when
we let go of our illusions of control

the fruits of the way
that flesh from our times of silence ...

Sr Bernadine Meskell has been a member of the enclosed Poor Clare Contemplative Order of nuns for the past forty-six years. She is currently Abbess of her community.

PEACE

I think peace has a lot to do with forsaking the addiction to the external. Sr Stanislaus sums this up beautifully in *Stillness Through my Prayers*, when she writes, '*Staying too close to affluence, my wants increase, vessels enlarge, rarely full, never enough. Staying close to the source of life, my needs diminish, vessels reduce, I am always full, overflowing with joy.*'

Living according to our own goals and following our hearts, is, I think, a crucial element in finding peace. Living according to the expectations of others is like living your life with a mask over your face, pretending to be something you are not, and will only lead to constant frustration. We need to take time to be quiet so that we can listen to the 'quiet voice within'.

I love Fintan O'Toole's piece, which follows, where he talks about having a grip on life that is tender yet firm. This applies so much to young children as they hit teenage years and young adulthood, but also applies to all of us, in our relationships with spouses, family and friends. We need to feel the support of the people around us, but not so much that we are suffocated and can't breathe. All of us need space to follow our own unique path, surrounded by the support and goodwill of those we love. To my mind, this is the path to inner peace.

FINTAN O'TOOLE

As I REMEMBER, THE FILM WAS CALLED SCARAMOUCHE, but it may well have been some other black-and-white swashbuckling epic. I don't remember anything else about it, but one scene has stayed with me for over forty years. The hero was a young and foppish French aristocrat who had been wronged in some way, and now had to learn to fight. He went to an old swordsman to take lessons. The old man's lines are the ones I remember: '*A sword in your hand, is like a bird. Hold it too loosely and it will fly away. Hold it too tightly and you will strangle it.*'

The lines stuck with me because they say something about happiness. We need, as human beings, things to hold on to. We need goals and ambitions and dreams. We need sex and love and affection. We need ideals and values and beliefs. Without them, we drift into the relentless succession of one damn thing after another. Instead of being a journey with a destination, life becomes a maze whose walls close in on us. We must hold on for dear life.

The trick, though, is finding the right kind of grip on the things we need. Holding on too tightly to specific ambitions makes the inevitable failures intolerable. Holding on too tightly to ideals and beliefs makes them curdle into rigid dogmas that have no place for life's contingencies and ambiguities. Holding on too tightly to life itself makes the inevitability of death fall like a constant shadow over its fleeting pleasures.

And so, I think of happiness as that bird in the hand, guarded carefully and closely, but cupped with a touch so delicate that its heart beats without panic and its breath comes easy.

Fintan O'Toole is Assistant Editor of The Irish Times, *for which he writes two weekly columns. His recent books include* White Savage: William Johnson and the Invention of America *and* The Irish Times Book of the 1916 Rising.

Bertie Ahern

I set out below a favourite quotation, and will, I hope, explain how it motivated me during my time as Taoiseach:

Human beings suffer
They torture one another,
They get hurt and they get hard.
No poem or play or song
Can fully right a wrong
Inflicted and endured.

The innocent in gaols
Beat on their bars together.
A hunger-striker's father
Stands in the graveyard dumb.
The police widow in veils
Faints at the funeral home

History says, Don't hope
On this side of the grave.
But then, once in a lifetime
The longed-for tidal wave
Of justice can rise up,
And hope and history rhyme.

So hope for a great sea-change
On the far side of revenge.
Believe that a further shore
Is reachable from here
Believe in miracle
And cures and healing wells.

Call the miracle self-healing:
The utter, self-revealing
Double-take of feeling.
If there's fire on the mountain
Or lightning and storm
And a god speaks from the sky

That means someone is healing
The outcry and the birth-cry
Of new life at its term.

from *The Cure at Troy: A Version of*
Sophocles' Philoctetes by
Seamus Heaney, 1991

This quotation is an excerpt from the writings of one of this island's most accomplished writers, Seamus Heaney, who was born in Derry, a city so long a symbol of the divisions and conflict on this island.

These words have become synonymous with the quest for peace on this island. Not long after becoming Taoiseach, I quoted from the same words, as did, on other occasions, former Prime Minister Blair and former President Clinton.

When I look back on my time as Taoiseach, I now realise how much of my waking hours (and quite a few sleepless nights) were dominated by bringing forward a solution to the conflict in Northern Ireland and then, in later years, by working equally hard to ensure that agreement was implemented. Northern Ireland would take up approximately forty hours of my working week, every week. And this was before I even started into all my other government, constituency and party duties!

I never regretted all the time I put into the Peace Process, even when, at times, we seemed to run into cul-de-sac after cul-de-sac. Seamus' words capture the need for persistence, and their inspiring message is never to give up and to keep striving for peace.

My motivation was rooted in the fact that the prize of peace was too valuable to the country to stop pursuing. Seamus' words had a real resonance for me and, I think, for all of us who shared that dream of building a new future on this island, grounded in harmony and friendship of all the people.

The words point to the futility of violence and the unstoppable momentum that came from the hopes of ordinary people for peace. And, for me, these words have real meaning because I entered politics in 1977, at a time when violence stalked the streets of Northern Ireland.

In the period since then, because of the conflict on this island, thousands of people died; thousands more were injured; thousands of families were left broken and grieving - without fathers and mothers, brothers or sisters. This happened on this island, in our lifetime. Whatever the circumstances, whatever the motivation, whatever the hurt felt before hurt was caused, none of that violence was justified.

On the day I was first elected Taoiseach, in June 1997, I said the historic task of our generation would be to finally heal the wounds of division that had festered for too long. Peace in Ireland is my proudest achievement. It is an achievement I share with thousands and thousands of people across this island and beyond our shores, who were voices for sanity, persuaders for justice and implacable opponents of those who sought to cling to violence as a political weapon.

The history of this island has been, at times, a blood-stained one, but thankfully we have now turned a page. In Seamus' eloquent words: *'Once again a lifetime/ The longed-for tidal wave/Of justice can rise up,/And hope and history rhyme.'*

Bertie Ahern retired as Taoiseach in May 2008, during his third term in office. He continues to serve as a member of Dáil Éireann. He played a pivotal part in the negotiations of the Good Friday Agreement. During his presidency of the European Council to June 2004, Bertie Ahern presided over the historic enlargement of the European Union to twenty-seven members. He has been the recipient of various honorary degrees by several universities, and is one of only five people to have been invited to address both the British Houses of Parliament and the House of Congress of the United States.

PATRICIA SCANLAN

There is a Destiny that makes us brothers: no one goes his way alone.
What we put in to the lives of others comes back
in to our own.

Edwin Markham

I WAS IN MY MID-TWENTIES, FLICKING through a magazine when I read Edwin Markham's famous quotation, and it really touched a chord. Probably for the first time in my life, it brought home to me the impact any actions of mine, good or bad, could have on someone else's life. I was, of course, aware of the Lord's decree: '*Do unto others as you would have them do unto you*', but something about Markham's quotation resonated deeply and I've tried ever since to hold on to it as a blueprint for my life.

In all my spiritual searching, the knowledge that we are all divine and all equal has been the most empowering message for me. No one is greater or lesser than the other. We each have our path in life, no matter how successful we may or may not consider ourselves to be. At the end of the day, it is not how materially or financially successful we are that is important, but how we have loved and allowed ourselves to be loved. And equally important, how much we have loved ourselves.

Most of us miss this very important teaching. You must love your neighbour as yourself. We feel guilty about loving ourselves or blowing our own trumpet. Our generation, and generations before us, were reared to a judgemental, even a wrathful God. Great emphasis was placed on our 'sins'. We were told we were not worthy.

Most religions teach us that we are not worthy, that we are inferior to our Creator. But this is so far from the truth. We have lost sight of how truly wonderful and special and magnificent we are. By our very divinity, we are most worthy. We are of the Creator. We have Divine DNA. How could we not be worthy? If we could all see each other's spiritual beauty and magnificence, how different our lives would be. By focusing on our negativities, religions have caused us to forget who and what we are. It is so important for us, in these terribly difficult days, to reconnect with our divinity and with each other. Not to concentrate on our failures, but on our successes and our joys: on family, friends and the beauty of the planet that has been placed in our care. If we turn dark thoughts to ones of gratitude, the energy of our life changes and it is much easier to stay positive.

Simple things, like watching a sunrise or a sunset, listening to the sea wash against the shore, seeing the sunlight filter through the trees, looking at the velvety petals of a rose, can help us pause from our busy lives and remind us of our gifts.

Watching a baby smile, seeing children playing, seeing the world through their eyes, with their purity and simplicity, we remember, if we were so blessed, our own carefree days of childhood. Children are wonderful teachers: they simplify everything and see the wonder of each other and the world as it should be seen. It is we, as adults, who create complications because of ego, greed, aggression and fear.

As I grow older, I find it is so much easier to let things go. I try to hand problems, over which I have no control, to the Divine to let Him sort it. It makes life much easier. If you can cultivate serenity amidst all the chaos of daily life, half the battle has been won. I try and visualise money as energy when I'm paying my bills, knowing that if you send the energy out with a blessing, it comes back to you. Like most people today, after years of hard work, my investments and pensions have taken a hammering because of the greed that is endemic in our world, but I'm trying to cope with it in the knowledge that I can lose nothing that is mine by Divine Right. Thinking like this is much less stressful than linking into the fear and negativity that is surrounding the global economy.

My twenty-year-old niece sent me this in a text when I was in hospital and feeling very down after major surgery:

> 'For I know what I have planned for you,' says the Lord. 'I have plans to prosper you, not to harm you. I have plans to give you a future filled with hope. When you call out to me and come to me in prayer, I will hear your prayers. When you seek me in prayer and

worship, you will find me available to you. If you seek me with all your heart and soul, I will make myself available to you,' says the Lord.

(Jeremiah 29:10-15)

It was such a thoughtful and loving gift from a wonderful young woman, who is a very precious gift to us in her own right. Now, when I pray, I try not to ask about the situation but ask for what God wants for me, as I figure that request can only have a win-win outcome!

I have learned that I never have to carry a burden alone, that when I ask for help, it is always forthcoming. But it won't come unless it is asked for, out of respect for the gift of free will we have been given. Our world is in upheaval, but we need not be, if we change our ways of thinking and doing and remember our divinity and who we really are.

Patricia Scanlan was born in Dublin, where she still lives. Her books, all number one bestsellers, include City Girl, Forgive and Forget, Happy Ever After, *and* Winter Blessings. *Her latest book, published in October 2009, is entitled* Coming Home. *Patricia is also Series Editor of the* Open Door *series, a prestigious literacy project she developed with New Island Publishers.*

Eamonn Lawlor

The great French composer, Hector Berlioz (1803-1869), in his brilliant memoirs, described his long walking trips as a young man in the Abruzzi mountains, east of Rome, and the flights of feeling and imagination – as well as the learning and growing self-awareness – of a great romantic artist coming into his own. The overwhelming passions of younger days are spiced in these pages (but not dimmed or denied) by a sharp, ironic wit, and his memoirs should inspire anyone who has ever struggled to hold heart and head in balance. And then there is the music ...

> Sometimes, when I had my guitar with me instead of my gun, I would station myself in the midst of a landscape in harmony with my mood, and some passage of the *Aeneid*, dormant in my memory since childhood, would come back to me ...

> Under the combined influence of poetry, music and association, I would work myself up into an incredible state of excitement. The triple intoxication always ended in floods of tears and uncontrollable sobbing. The most curious part of it was that I was able to

analyse my feelings. I wept for poor Turnus, robbed by the hypocrite Aeneas of kingdom, mistress and life. I wept for the beautiful and pathetic Lavinia, forced to wed an unknown brigand with her lover's blood still fresh upon him. I longed for those poetic days when the heroes, sons of the gods, walked the earth in glittering armour, casting delicate javelins, their points set in a ring of gleaming gold. Quitting the past for the present, I wept for my own private disappointments, my uncertain future, my interrupted career: until, collapsing amid this maelstrom of poetry, and murmuring snatches of Shakespeare, Virgil and Dante: '*Nessun maggior dolore* ... *che ricordarsi* ... *Oh poor Ophelia* ... '*Good night, sweet ladies*' ... *Vitaque cum gemitu* ... *fugit indignata* ... *sub umbras*' – I fell asleep.

What madness, many will say. Yes, but what happiness. Sensible people have no idea what it is to have this intense consciousness simply of being alive.

from *The Memoirs of Hector Berlioz*, translated by
David Cairns, 2002

Eamonn Lawlor presents The Lyric Concert *on weekday evenings on RTÉ Lyric FM. Previously an RTÉ journalist, he was the station's European correspondent in the 1980s, and subsequently presented news programmes on television, including* Six One News *and* Primetime.

TONY WARD

Message for Life

BACK IN THE LATE 1960S/EARLY 1970s, my place of study was at an old Singer sewing machine located in the spare bedroom in my grandparents' house in Harold's Cross, Dublin 6. As much as I would like to give the impression of conscientious preparation for the Intermediate and Leaving Cert., the reality was more that of needs must, with the following day's 'ecker' (homework) the be all and end all to 'sewing machine' work.

There was one saving grace, however, and it came in the shape of a tiny, badly battered, old transistor radio. The reception was appalling, and the crackling irritating in the extreme. It was, however, my night-time link with the outside world. Few stations were clearly audible; some slightly better than others. Radio Luxembourg was one of those. It was broadcast on medium wave 208.

It was our mobile phone, laptop, Blackberry, texting, e-mail, YouTube, Facebook - every modern-day communications gizmo you care to name, rolled into one. Luxembourg was compulsive listening, particularly for 'with it' teens. Every hour, on the hour, they ran the '208 Powerplay', 'Make me an Island', by the late, great Joe Dolan was one tracks they played. I loved it and, God, was Joe cool back then. But the track that blew me away the very first time I heard it was by an unknown artist called Les Crane.

'Desiderata' never made it to number one, but, as a message for life, it registered, and to this day has stayed with me. It provides the measure by which I have always tried to live my life, and the values to which I would like to think we as a family - individually and collectively - adhere.

This wonderful message, which begins: *'Go placidly amid the noise and the haste/And remember what peace there may be in silence'*, was not, as was mooted at the time, found scribbled on a piece of paper beneath a headstone in Old St Paul's Church in the seventeenth century, but was in fact written by Max Ehrmann in the 1920s. It encapsulates for me the journey through life in the most balanced and most realistic way. It recognizes human frailties, but suggests means of discovering ways around them. Pressure of space prevents me reproducing all forty-five lines of this wonderful message here, and more's the pity, because each line is loaded and very, very special in its own right.

I do beg editorial licence, however, in highlighting one or two key segments:

> If you compare yourself with others,
>   you may become vain or bitter,

for always there will be greater and
lesser persons than yourself.
Enjoy your achievements as well as your plans.
Keep interested in your own career,
however humble;
it is a real possession in the changing
fortunes of time.

Take kindly the counsel of the years,
gracefully surrendering the youth

You are a child of the universe
no less than the trees and the stars;
you have a right to be here

With all its sham, drudgery, and broken dreams,
it is still a beautiful world.
Be cheerful. Strive to be happy.

The theme is contentment, achieved through '*peace with God/whatever you conceive Him to be*'. The poem has adorned the walls of my home in various places over more years than I care to remember. It has provided me with solace in times of darkness and despair. It has guided me through my sporting career every bit as much as my day-to-day living. I find it inspirational and motivational in equal measure. It is low on dogma, but high on optimism. It captures for me what life, for all its twists and turns, is in essence all about.

I am not an overly philosophical or hugely religious person but, that beautifully crafted musical version of Ehrmann's poem on that badly battered old tranny all those years ago has provided me with something tangible and meaningful to which to retreat in times of crisis over the course of my life. When, in the words of the singer songwriter James Taylor: 'you're down and troubled and you need a helping hand' – well, in 'Desiderata', you've got the consummate friend. Try it yourself: you won't be disappointed.

Tony Ward was a rugby union and soccer player during the 1970s and 1980s. He played rugby as a fly-half for a number of teams, including Munster, Leinster, Ireland, the British and Irish Lions, and the Barbarians. He also played soccer for both Shamrock Rovers and Limerick United. In 1981, he played for Limerick United against Southampton, and helped them win the FAI Cup in 1982. Since retiring as a sportsman, he has worked as a sports journalist and as a rugby commentator for RTÉ.

DELIA CONLON

Grove of Tranquillity

THE WORLD TODAY IS SO FULL of disturbance, disruption and distraction that we all need a little break to refresh our mental process and get back on an even keel. It is just not possible to keep going at breakneck speed from morning to night, day after day.

When I go into my garden, it is, for me, a journey in time. For me, it represents a lifetime of activity, sometimes hard work and knowledge gained, and still accumulating. The most interesting season is Spring. After a few months of inactivity, everything is rousing from slumber and coming back to life, to begin a new season of growth and reproduction. Progress is apparent every day, buds appear, bursting into leaf and flower. Seeds sown appear above the earth and gradually assume the expected form. It is not all plain sailing. Enemies are at work too. Birds can eat the seeds I have sown. Slugs can eat newly emerging leaves and the insect world also comes to life. Aphids attack all sorts of plants, and the aphids themselves are eaten by certain wasps and ladybirds. It is exciting and challenging to keep on top of all the activity.

For as long as I can remember, I have had a love of garden-ing. But when I moved into my own house, many years ago, I received advice from a lady who had been tending a very beautiful garden for most of her life. She gave me a book on gardening, which, in its first chapter, advised me to start at the beginning, by testing the soil for pH, nitrogen, phosphate and potash, in order to see what nutrients were needed. This all sounded much too scientific for me. All I wanted was to plant a few shrubs and flowers. In that, I have had many successes and a few failures. I have learned a lot by trial and error. The garden has matured a little each year, and now provides the protection I need against all the distractions of life. Exotic plants from the tropics have to be protected from the frosts of winter, but grow very well in my garden in summer. Scented plants exude exquisite perfume as the shadows lengthen, and the barbecue, with a bottle of wine on a summer evening provides a Heaven on earth. When I sit in the garden in the dappled shade as the sun is setting, it is so peaceful and calm. I think of that line, in Yeats' lovely poem, '*Aedh Wishes from the Cloths of Heaven*': '*Of night and light and the half light.*'

Delia Conlon grew up on a farm in Kilnamona, Co. Clare, and went on to a career in nursing in the UK, Ireland and the United States. She married Dublin GP, Dr Peter Conlon, and they have seven children, four of whom also studied medicine. Delia's lega-cy to her children is faith, an abiding confidence in themselves and a wonderful childhood.

CECILY KELLEHER

WHEN I WAS FIRST APPOINTED TO the Chair of Health Promotion at NUI Galway, I was still very young, had just one infant son and was attempting to distil a long period of rigorous and scientifically sceptical medical training into a model of health and well being that was more expansive, embracing and to which people in their everyday lives could to relate.

Over a decade or so, I worked very hard as an academic and a mother, learning as much as teaching, and what I was seeking most was to combine the practical with the theoretical. When I advocated that the key to good health and well being was personal control, what did I mean? It was so important to rise above the banal jargon, if a meaningful message was to get across. The basic gist was that people who felt they had discretion in emotional, financial or physical decisions in their lives made better personal health choices – whether in their lifestyles or the use of services – than people who did not. The more I learned that this was not always personally possible for me in every aspect of my own life, and that I was as flawed as everyone else, the more nuanced my message became.

Some practise such discretion at a personal or spiritual level. Some are so challenged by the obstacles of their social position that they rebel or reject the messages of the system that alienates them. Some effortlessly assimilate change and achieve measurable health benefits to enjoy long and healthy lives. There is no 'one size that fits all' in health promotion, and no single champion or philosopher to guide the way. It is a process rather than a prescribed pathway.

For me, that process includes a curiosity to understand health and society in a highly contextual way. What is it like to be an Irish person living now? How does this relate both to other contemporaries across the globe and to Irish people in the past? Over the past six years at University College Dublin, my work has taken on this focus. The diaspora has proven a key to this enquiry. Irish people abroad suffered great deprivation and social struggle, and manifested much poorer health than others, often with even less affluent lifestyles. The health gains at home and abroad have been achieved by improved health care, especially for mothers and children, but also by other forms of empowerment, through improved living conditions, channelling of positive life characteristics and lifestyles, and a sense of belonging to the global community that worked to contribute to our national sense of self-esteem in a constructive way.

The most important lesson for us today is that there is no utopian ideal from the past, or indeed for the future: no easy fix. Principles of social justice and opportunity will help to underpin what is needed to maintain possibilities for the future for all our children, and those who feel supported and cared for will indeed survive best. My infant son, as was, is now a student of Chinese and his baby brother spent his transition year in Spain. We must not fear the future: that is like saying we fear our own selves, which is manifestly not true.

Cecily Kelleher is Professor of Public Health Medicine and Epidemiology at University College Dublin.

LUKE DRURY

I would encourage any young person with an enquiring mind to seriously consider studying science, not necessarily as a career - although that is certainly a possibility - but just for the intellectual excitement of taking part in one of the great human endeavours. The natural sciences are peculiarly satisfying, because they deliver real insight into how the world actually works, insights that are verifiable (or perhaps more accurately, if one follows Popper, 'falsifiable') by observation and experiment, and thus in some sense reflect an objective, external reality.

To discover some new fact about how the world is put together, something that nobody knew before, even in a small way, is an amazingly satisfying experience. Nor does this in any way diminish the wonder and grandeur of the universe: on the contrary, the more we understand the world, the more beautiful and strange, and yet in some sense inevitable, it appears. Of course, science is not easy, but nothing really worthwhile is, and its discoveries are truly more permanent than bronze.

Luke Drury studied Experimental Physics and Pure Mathematics at Trinity College Dublin, before doing a PhD in Astrophysics at Cambridge University England. He worked in the Max-Planck-Institut für Kernphysik, Heidelberg from 1979-1986, returning to Dublin in 1986 as a Senior Professor at the Dublin Institute for Advanced Studies.

CHRISTINA NOBLE

CHILDREN'S

FOUNDATION

If you would like to make a donation to the
Christina Noble Children's Foundation,
please contact our office:

22 South Frederick Street,
Dublin 2
Ireland
Ph: 01 645 5555
Email: Ireland@cncf.ie
www.cncf.org

Acknowledgements/Permissions

The Publishers and the Author gratefully acknowledge permission to include the following copyright material: 'A Christmas Childhood', from *A Soul for Sale and Other Poems*, 1947, and 'In Memory of My Mother' by Patrick Kavanagh, reprinted by kind permission of the Trustees of the Estate of the late Katherine B. Kavanagh, through the Jonathan Williams Literary Agency; 'Perspectives' by Louis Mulcahy, copyright ©2009, by permission of Louis Mulcahy; 'Digging' from *Death of a Naturalist*, (Faber & Faber, 1966), 'St Kevin and the Blackbird' from *The Spirit Level* (Faber & Faber, 1996) and from The Cure at Troy: A Version of Sophocles' Philoctetes (FSG, 1991; Faber & Faber 2002) by Seamus Heaney, reprinted by kind permission of Seamus Heaney and Faber & Faber Ltd; 'Nature as Art' by Ann Henning Jocelyn, copyright ©2009, by permission of Ann Henning Jocelyn; Extracts from *Divine Beauty* and *Anam Cara* by John O'Donoghue (Bantam Books/Bantam Press, 2003; 1997), reprinted by kind permission of the Random House Group Ltd.; Extract from *Memoirs of Hector Berlioz* by Hector Berlioz, edited by E. Newman, translated by R.E. Holmes, translation copyright 1932 by Alfred A. Knopf, a division of Random House, Inc and renewed 1960 by Vera Newman: used by permission of Alfred A. Knopf, a division of Random House, Inc.; 'Mystery' from *Stillness through my Prayers* by Sr Stanislaus Kennedy, published by Transworld Ireland (2009), and reprinted by permission of the Random House Group Ltd.;'Malaga, O Malaga' by Rita Ann Higgins copyright ©2009, by permission of Rita Ann Higgins; 'Always Look On The Bright Side of Life' Words and Music by Eric Idle © 1979, Reproduced by permission of EMI Virgin Music Ltd, W8 5SW.; From *Keylines*